THE REAGAN WIT

★ THE ★
REAGAN
WIT

★ ★ ★

THE HUMOR OF
THE AMERICAN PRESIDENT

EDITED BY

Bill Adler and Bill Adler, Jr.

WILLIAM MORROW AND COMPANY, INC.

NEW YORK

It is the policy of William Morrow and Company, Inc., and its imprints and affiliates, recognizing the importance of preserving what has been written, to print the books we publish on acid-free paper, and we exert our best efforts to that end.

Library of Congress Cataloging-in-Publication Data
Reagan, Ronald.
    The Reagan wit : the humor of the American president / edited by
Bill Adler and Bill Adler, Jr.
        p.   cm.
    ISBN 0-688-15514-6
    1. Reagan, Ronald—Humor. 2. Reagan, Ronald—Quotations.
    3. Reagan, Ronald—Anecdotes. I. Adler, Bill. II. Adler, Bill,
1956–   . III. Title.
E877.2.R423 1997
973.927'092—dc21   97-30824
                                                         CIP

Printed in the United States of America

First Edition

1   2   3   4   5   6   7   8   9   10

BOOK DESIGN BY ELLEN CIPRIANO

www.williammorrow.com

With love
for Karen, Madeleine, Claire, and Amanda

Contents

Introduction   ix

CHAPTER 1: The Early Years   1

CHAPTER 2: The Campaign for Governor   11

CHAPTER 3: The Years as Governor   21

CHAPTER 4: The Years in Between   71

CHAPTER 5: Reagan Looks at Reagan   79

CHAPTER 6: The Campaign for President, 1976   91

CHAPTER 7: The Campaign for President, 1980   99

CHAPTER 8: The Presidency   127

CHAPTER 9: The Assassination Attempt   175

CHAPTER 10: After the Presidency   187

Introduction

It would be impossible to successfully assume the responsibilities of the presidency without a keen sense of humor. Ronald Wilson Reagan, the fortieth President of the United States, goes down in history as one of our wittiest leaders, with a remarkable ability to make his audiences feel at ease. Reagan's gibes and clever one-liners were instrumental to him in winning the hearts of the American people throughout his political career. From his early days as a college student through his years as an actor, as governor of the most populous state in the Union, and finally as President of the United States, Ronald Reagan has always been known for his comic timing and for his knack for graceful chiding. Reagan not only loves to make people laugh by poking fun at himself and the world around him, but also knows how to use wit to defend himself and the ideas he believes in.

The Reagan Wit offers anecdotes, humorous stories, and

quips that span nearly all of Reagan's life, presenting a penetrating and fascinating insight into the man, his personality, and his beliefs. A collection of the humor for which Reagan is so well known and well loved, *The Reagan Wit* paints a memorable portrait of this magnificent man.

—BILL ADLER AND BILL ADLER, JR.

THE REAGAN WIT

The Early Years

Ronald Reagan has been entertaining people with his jokes and anecdotes ever since his early days as a student at Eureka College, and it is in those early years that we see the beginnings of the delightful Reagan wit. Considered a very likable person by virtually everyone who came into contact with him, he was also known to be a genuinely funny individual with a unique sense of humor.

His wit not only helped him make it through some difficult moments in college but also proved invaluable in his careers as a radio sportscaster, in the Army, and later as a movie star. Ronald Reagan made many people laugh in those early years and continued to entertain them throughout his political career, often incorporating anecdotes about his life as a young man into his speeches. It was during his years as an actor and later president of the Screen Actors Guild that Reagan became involved in the fight against communism. His humor presents excellent insight into the evolution of Reagan's career from Hollywood to politics and the many beliefs and conceptions that came to play an important part in his role as President.

Of his early family life, growing up in Dixon, Illinois, Ronald Reagan once said:

Our family didn't exactly come from the wrong side of the tracks, but we were certainly always within the sound of the train whistles.

As a teenager, Reagan worked in the summers as a lifeguard. Recalling those days, he wrote:

The only money I ever got was ten dollars for diving for an old man's upper plate that he lost going down our slide.

At Eureka College, the former President was a tackle on the football team, an experience he would relish and look back on nostalgically for the rest of his life. Of those days, he wrote:

The lure of sweat and action always pulled me back to the game—despite the fact that I was a scrawny, undersized, underweight nuisance, who insisted on getting in the way of the more skillful (such as my brother). As a result, I had a collection of the largest purplish-black bruises possible. More than once, I must have been a walking coagulation. Those were the happiest times of my life.

As a young man, Reagan once parked his Model T Ford near a lamppost, which he climbed. Soon after, a police officer drove up to the younger Reagan and asked him what he was doing up there. Reagan replied:

Twinkle, twinkle, little star, just who do you think you are?

Reagan was fined a dollar.

Reagan was once stricken with viral pneumonia so badly, he recalls that he almost decided to stop breathing, but a nurse persuaded him to take another breath and, according to Reagan:

She was *so* nice and persistent that I let her have her way.

Remembering his days as a high school student, Reagan once said:

I have a warm spot for school principals. I was in the principal's office once in Dixon High School, and I wasn't there just to pass the time of day. Well, at one point he said to me, "You know, I don't care what you think of me now, I'm only interested in what you think of me fifteen years from now."

About his first trip to Chicago, Reagan said:

I couldn't afford cabs and I was afraid of the damn buses—as a matter of fact, the city itself scared the bejesus out of me. Everybody seemed to know where they were going and what they were doing, and I could get lost just looking for a men's room.

When Montgomery Ward turned Reagan down for a job in the 1930s, he decided to leave town and look for a position as a radio announcer. According to Reagan, it was a blessing that he wasn't hired at the store. As he said years later:

I was about as low as I could be. Many times, I thought, had I got the job in the Montgomery Ward store, I probably still would be working there.

As a freshman at Eureka College, Reagan led a protest against budget cuts proposed by the school's president. Referring to this as the first time he had ever tried to incite political action, Reagan said:

I discovered that night that an audience has a feel to it and, in the parlance of theater, that audience and I were together. When I came to actually presenting the motion there was no need for parliamentary procedure; they came to their feet with a roar; even the faculty members present voted by acclamation.

When Reagan was just setting out on his career as an actor, he received an urgent telegram from his agent, Bill Meilkjohn:

WARNER'S OFFER CONTRACT SEVEN YEARS, ONE YEAR'S OPTIONS, STARTING AT $200 A WEEK. WHAT SHALL I DO?

He shot back his reply:

SIGN BEFORE THEY CHANGE THEIR MINDS.

Regarding the situation in Hollywood in the 1950s, Reagan re-monstrated in 1956:

A lot of the crying sounds coming out of our studios today are like a guy sitting on a nail, too lazy to get up from what's hurting him.

In another story about his acting career, Reagan joked about one of his less successful movies:

In those days American motion pictures occupied more than 75 percent of the playing time of all the screens in the world. Unfortunately the movies that we sent overseas sometimes—well, they weren't always successful. I had one called *Cattle Queen of Montana.* It lost something in Japanese.

Referring to his Army career, Reagan quipped about his bad eyesight:

Colonel Ferguson turned me over to the adjutant at Fort Mason on the first day of my military service. I discovered that, even though I was in, another physical was required. I went through the same old business with the eyes, and one of the two examining doctors said, "If we sent you overseas, you'd shoot at a general."

The other doctor looked up and said, "Yes, and you'd miss him."

On acting:

Today, however, if I could give one bit of advice to youngsters starting out in theater or the movies I'd say: Don't marry your leading lady or leading man until you've done another role opposite someone else. Leading lady: It is an infatuation that won't hold up once the play is over and you each go back to playing yourselves.

Reagan appeared in many movies during his acting career. Regarding those films, he wrote:

The studio didn't want good—it wanted them Thursday.

Reagan commented about another of his films:

I saw *Knute Rockne* one night, and it was so hacked up, my eighty-yard run was a five-yard loss.

From early on, Reagan took a stand against communism. While a member of the Screen Actors Guild, he said:

There has been a small clique within the Screen Actors Guild which has consistently opposed the policies of the guild board and officers of the guild. . . . That small clique . . . has been suspected of more or less following the tactics that we associate with the Communist party.

When trying to convince his daughter Maureen of the benefits of an education, Reagan drew from his own experience in Hollywood. Charming her into an affection for her studies, Reagan told Maureen that in order to become an actress herself, she had to learn to read and write:

[To] be able to sign contracts and give autographs [and read scripts].

CHAPTER 2

The Campaign for Governor

Ronald Reagan was elected governor of California in 1966 as a result of his own formidable political abilities and of former Governor Pat Brown's waning public support. But in addition to his superb political strategy, which struck a chord with an increasing number of Americans, Reagan also won the hearts of the American public and the media through his jokes and stories, which, told casually and often, became an essential tool of his campaign, launched in 1965.

In this first political campaign, Reagan used his jabs much as a fine fencer wields a saber. The American public fell in love with his ability to cajole, and Reagan's political career began.

Of his new political career, Reagan said in a speech on March 30, 1966, in California's Orange County:

Suddenly now that I want to be something else besides an actor, everybody is saying that I'm an actor. I'll probably be the only fellow who will get an Oscar posthumously.

Following is a response to one of the many letters Reagan received:

January 13, 1966

Mrs. Smith Ely Jelliffe

Dear Mrs. Jelliffe:

Thanks very much for your letter. Unfortunately it didn't arrive in time to save me. I am now a candidate for governor.

Let's just put it this way. We'll give the Republicans one more chance to see whether they'd rather fight than vote. If they don't reform, I'll join you in your retirement from politics and you can teach me the pleasures of wondering.

Best regards,
Ronald Reagan

Reagan commented during a drive past Disneyland:

In my position, you know, you can't just wander around. You are a tourist attraction yourself.

When asked what his main campaign issue was during his first campaign for governor, Reagan quipped:

To retire Pat Brown.

—1966

Reagan responded to the charge that he had no political experience:

I don't know of anybody who was born holding office. I am not a professional politician. The man who currently has the job has more political experience than anybody. That's why I'm running.

Comments on Governor Pat Brown:

Keeping up with Governor Brown's promises is like reading *Playboy* magazine while your wife turns the pages.

—1966

Well, he's good to his family . . . he's put a lot of relatives on the payroll.

The governor talks about *his* dams and *his* lakes and *his* reservoirs; you have the feeling that when he leaves office he'll take them with him.

—1966

I have an opponent who says money is the mother's milk of politics, and you've never seen a baby who has so much squawk about where the milk comes from.

Although many assumed that Reagan would soon issue a formal declaration of his candidacy, the then noncandidate said:

I've also said, of course, you keep one foot back in case the sky starts to fall.

—1965

On campaigning in general:

President Dewey warned me not to get overconfident.

—1966

Reagan met many famous people in his lifetime and often incorporated his experiences with them into his speeches. In a story about Jimmy Stewart, Reagan once told an audience:

[Jimmy] would introduce me at various banquets along the campaign trail, and every time the emcee introduced him, he would talk about his great stardom in the pictures. Each time I got up, I would . . . add . . . that [Jimmy] not only flew the Hamburg run, but that he was a major general in the Air Corps Reserve.

One time, after several of these situations, the master of ceremonies did refer to Jimmy's military record and then said, "Brigadier General Jimmy Stewart." So when I got up, I apologized to the emcee . . . and said, "It's Major General Jimmy Stewart."

That night when we got back to the hotel, Jimmy said, "Ron, that fellow was right, it is brigadier general. I just never corrected you before because it sounded so good."

On what it would be like for an actor to become governor of California:

I don't know—I've never played governor before.

—August 3, 1965

Reagan's conservative philosophy of government is well known; in fact it triggered a political revolution. His less-is-better approach was often presented by means of colorful figures of speech:

Government is like a baby—an alimentary canal with a big appetite on one end and no sense of responsibility at the other.

—1965

Once upon a time, the only contact with government was when you went to buy a stamp.

—1965

Politics is just like show business. You need a big opening. Then you coast for a while. Then you need a big finish.

Referring to liberals, Reagan commented:

The labels somehow got pasted on the wrong people.

On defending our political system against communism, Reagan once told an audience that the need to fight is immediate:

If they were so complacent as to think they could sit back and not lift a hand until the battle involved them personally, they were about as shortsighted as a fellow going into the poultry business without a rooster—they were putting a hell of a lot of confidence in the stork.

Recalling his days as a "hemophiliac liberal," Reagan wrote in his autobiography:

I have come to realize that a great many so-called liberals aren't liberal—they will defend to the death your right to agree with them.

We are told that God is dead. Well, He isn't. We just can't talk to Him in the classroom anymore.

As a candidate, Reagan took issue with pornography in California:

The biggest joke in Paris, France, is that instead of selling French postcards, they're selling California postcards.

—1966

Speaking in the vegetable-growing region of California to a group of women, Reagan pointed out his concern over the high cost of living:

You ladies know that if you stand in front of the asparagus counter at the supermarket these days, it's cheaper to eat money.

Reagan occasionally joked about the charge that he received support from the John Birch Society and other ultraconservative groups, and often would begin his speeches by saying:

Gentlemen—and little ladies in tennis shoes.

—1966

While on the subject of conservation—a subject that has been dear to me for many years and on which I have spoken and written from the heart many times—I feel impelled, at this time, to express my animosity toward what I call "plinkers." In referring to "plinkers," I do not by any means mean the serious hunter in search of game; I mean those people who, with gun in hand, and no serious purpose in mind, get an itch to pull a trigger and "plink," there goes a robin or an oriole. Just because they wondered: "Could I?"

—1965

CHAPTER 3

The Years as Governor

As he made the career change from movie star to governor of California, Ronald Reagan entertained audiences with the parallels he drew between politics and Hollywood. There is no doubt that his comic gifts also helped him in dealing with the endless problems encountered in governing one of the nation's most populous states, and the numerous individuals he met each day as governor.

His eight-year term (1967–1975) coincided with the turbulent late 1960s and early '70s, a time when the nation

and California were torn by an undeclared war, campus un-
rest, open experimentation with drugs and sex, and a general
feeling of lack of national direction. In this first position in
his new, political career, Reagan's sense of humor served him
well as he fought to protect his administration and state
from disorder.

INAUGURATION AND FIRST DAYS AS GOVERNOR

At his midnight gubernatorial inauguration, Reagan remarked to the state's other show business politician, dancer-turned-senator George Murphy:

George, here we are on the late show again.

—JANUARY 3, 1967

Soon after he was elected governor, Reagan's campaign staff left. Reagan said to his then press secretary, Lyn Nofziger:

My God, what do we do now?

—1967

Concerning the regimen he suddenly found himself forced to fol-low, Reagan joked:

I wasn't quite prepared for a schedule that's more strict and busier than a baby's formula.

But Reagan made a smooth transition from acting to politics, noting:

Politics is just like show business.

On Reagan's first day as governor, candy maker Henry Rowland gave him a bag of jelly beans, which Reagan put on the Cabinet Room table. So began Reagan's tradition of passing out his favor-ite candy at Cabinet meetings. As Reagan later said to Rowland:

We can hardly start a meeting or make a decision with-out passing around the jar of jelly beans.

Soon after assuming the governorship, Reagan was faced with a hostile press. He remarked:

If this has been a honeymoon, then I've been sleeping alone.
—1967

Looking back at his first few months as governor, Reagan joked:

There was a time back around January when I felt like an Egyptian tank driver with a set of Russian instructions.

—1967

When I was first governor it seemed like every day brought more and more problems, but one day I was on the way to the office when I heard a disc jockey who became a great favorite of mine. Out of the clear blue sky he said, "Everybody should take unto himself a wife, because sooner or later something is bound to happen you can't blame on the governor."

Reagan on one of the difficulties he encountered soon after assuming the governorship:

I tried to dial a prayer and they hung up on me!

—1967

Upon his election as governor of California:

Nancy and I agreed, my new job made everything we'd ever done before seem as dull as dishwater.

On Big Government

Reagan on Democratic fund-raisers:

I've never been able to understand how the Democrats can run those $1,000-a-plate dinners at such a profit, and run the government at such a loss.

—Dallas, Texas,
October 26, 1967

Reagan was adamantly opposed to too much governmental regulation, as the following ironic comments make abundantly clear:

Fleas are a part of the ecological cycle, but I doubt if a dog thinks he is doing something to destroy ecology by wearing a flea collar.

Heaven help us if the government ever gets into the business of protecting us from ourselves.

—April 12, 1973

Referring to his appointment of people without governmental experience while he was governor, Reagan said:

There was a reason for my seeking people who didn't want government careers. Dr. Parkinson summed it all up in his book on bureaucracy. He said, "Government hires a rat-catcher and the first thing you know, he's become a rodent control officer."

—MARCH 31, 1976

Referring to the Democrats, Reagan commented:

The difference between them and us is that *we* want to check government spending, and *they* want to spend government checks.

Under [federal] regulations, for example, in Connecticut a sixth-grade boys' choir, long a tradition in the community, was forced to disband because it violated the HEW guidelines against sex discrimination. They say that musical groups can only be divided now on a basis of vocal range; but in the sixth grade the boys still sing soprano!

When government uses its coercive power to intervene in the free marketplace, agriculture can discover it has something worse to contend with than the corn borer or the boll weevil.

—DECEMBER 11, 1972

Government does not solve problems; it subsidizes them.

—December 11, 1972

In a letter to Nelson Rockefeller, Reagan wrote:

Dear Nelson:

Thanks very much for the autographed copy of your book, which I found awaiting me. I'm looking forward to reading it just as soon as I can get about 600 d—n bills signed, most of which could be left unsigned with great benefit to the people of Calif.

I'll see you in Miami. Again thanks.

Best regards,
Ron
—1968

Too many people, especially in government, feel that the nearest thing to eternal life we will ever see on this earth is a government program.

—May 10, 1972

Americans have had their night on the town of social tinkering and social experimentation. They are now suffering the morning after, and they are hungry for some good old ham and eggs fiscal common sense.

You might be weary of me sounding the same alarms. You might think, well, we have heard all this before, but somehow we muddled through. Well, this is like the window-washer who fell from the Empire State Building. When he passed the twentieth floor, he said, "So far, so good."

—OCTOBER 29, 1972

In a speech to the U.S. Chamber of Commerce, Reagan said:

In some dim beginning, man created the institution of government as a convenience for himself. And ever since that time, government has been doing its best to become an inconvenience. Government bureaus and agencies take on a life and purpose of their own. But I wonder if it happens because so many of us—all of us probably—read and hear and just repeat what we think is a truism: that when a public problem develops, government is forced to step in. That is utter nonsense. Government can hardly wait to step in. As a matter of fact, government is in the position of the fellow who will make a speech at the drop of a hat.

—WASHINGTON, D.C.
SEPTEMBER 24, 1972

Reagan on welfare:

I fear that with the best of intentions, with only a desire to help those less fortunate, we are making a god of government. A Samaritan crossed over the road and helped the beaten pilgrim himself—he did not report the case to the nearest welfare agency.

If the Interstate Commerce Commission had been in business during the pioneer days, the forty-niners would still be trying to find out what the rules are for crossing the Mississippi River.

—OCTOBER 15, 1974

ON PRESIDENTIAL ASPIRATIONS

A reporter once asked Reagan:

The Gallup poll shows that your popularity as a potential presidential candidate is slipping. How do you explain that?

Reagan replied:
I regard that as a tribute to my efforts to convince people that I'm not a candidate.

—1967

When asked about Nelson Rockefeller's presidential aspirations, Reagan said:

You're asking the wrong noncandidate. Ask him.

General William Tecumseh Sherman, in a telegram to the Republican National Convention in 1884, had replied to the convention's attempt to draft him:
IF NOMINATED, I WILL NOT ACCEPT. IF ELECTED, I WILL NOT SERVE.
When speculation increased about Reagan's becoming a candidate for the Republican nomination for President, a reporter asked if he would issue a Shermanesque statement. Reagan replied:

I never found anyone but Sherman who ever said that, so I figure it's his line.

—1968

Of his political aspirations, Reagan said:

The thought of being President frightens me and I do not think I want the job.

—1973

On Government and Politics
in General

When a reporter questioned him about the qualifications of his appointees, Reagan responded:

If I appointed him, he's qualified.

—1967

When the entire gubernatorial staff showed up for work on Lincoln's birthday, while most other state employees did not, Reagan quipped:

I just invited them to the party. They didn't *have* to come.

—1967

A computer error brought Reagan's Democratic predecessor, Edmund G. "Pat" Brown, a Republican fund-raising letter

*signed by Governor Ronald Reagan. The following correspon-
dence resulted:*

Dear Hon. Reagan:

In today's mail I received a letter from you recalling the
days of the Brown-Unruh clique.

I am very interested in your record of increased taxa-
tion, increased welfare costs and property taxes.

I really believe that Edmund G. Brown, Jr., will do a
far better job than your hand-picked candidate, Houston
Flournoy. I must, therefore, refuse your kind invitation to
contribute to the Republican State Central Committee.

Sincerely,
Edmund G. Brown

Reagan responded:

Dear Pat:

I just thought that you might be ready to do penance.

Sincerely,
Ronald W. Reagan

At a Republican fund-raising dinner, Reagan said:

Two and a half years ago we put a new captain [President Nixon] on the barnacle-encrusted ship of state. And now, the people who allowed that ship to become encrusted and swerve off course blame the captain for not providing an instant moonlight cruise.

—FRAMINGHAM, MASSACHUSETTS
JUNE 14, 1971

Reagan on crime:

One way to make sure crime doesn't pay would be to let the government run it.

—DALLAS, TEXAS
OCTOBER 26, 1967

In his inauguration address at the start of his second term as governor, Reagan said:

When those who are governed do too little, those who govern can—and often will—do too much.

—SACRAMENTO, CALIFORNIA
JANUARY 4, 1971

On some of the contradictions and ironies of political life:

There are some days you go home so frustrated that you get in the shower and you make speeches to the walls of the shower. But there are other days when you go home and feel ten feet tall because you have solved a problem.

I have learned that one of the most important rules in politics is poise—which means looking like an owl after you have behaved like a jackass.

They [those responsible for Watergate] did something that was stupid and foolish and was criminal—it was illegal. Illegal is a better word than criminal, because I think criminal has a different connotation. I think the tragedy of this is that men who are not criminals at heart, and certainly not engaged in criminal activities, committed a criminal or illegal act and now must bear the consequences. These are men whose lives are being very much changed by this. I doubt if any of them would even intentionally double-park.

—SACRAMENTO, CALIFORNIA
MAY 1, 1973

On two of his Democratic rivals:

Bobby Kennedy is making Lyndon Johnson so nervous he's thinking of putting the country in his wife's name.

—DALLAS, TEXAS
OCTOBER 26, 1967

Jesse Unruh was the opposition leader in the California legislature while Reagan was governor. In a letter to Lieutenant Governor Robert Finch, who was going to take charge of the state during the governor's absence, Reagan added a P.S.:

Bob, I'd like you to have the cornerstone of the new mansion laid by my return. Preferably with Jesse Unruh in it.

When briefed before drawing up his first state budget, Reagan quipped:

What I have recently learned about the state of finances in California, we may turn out to be the first state that ever ran on Diners Club cards.

—1967

There's an old legend about the politician who looks out his window and sees his constituents marching by. "There go my people," he says. "I must hasten to find out where they're going so I can get in front and lead them."

In the final days of his administration, Governor Pat Brown made eighty judicial appointments. About this Reagan lamented:

I'm probably the only governor who can't fix a parking ticket.

*When asked if he would approve a withholding tax bill in Cali-
fornia, Reagan replied:*

[Only] if they held a hot iron to my feet and I was
bound hand and foot.

—1967

If a bureaucrat had been writing the Ten Commandments, a simple rock slab would not have been near
enough room.

Those simple rules would have read: "Thou shalt not,
unless you feel strongly to the contrary, or for the following stated exceptions, see paragraphs 1–10, subsection
no. A."

—JUNE 6, 1974

*When asked what impact the candidacy of Senator Eugene
McCarthy would have on President Johnson's prospects for re-
election, Reagan said:*

This is the type of McCarthyism I heartily approve of—
anything that's divisive among Democrats is constructive to
Republicans.

—YALE UNIVERSITY
NEW HAVEN, CONNECTICUT
1967

When asked by a reporter whether he would look with an open mind at a particular bill before the California legislature, Reagan replied:

Oh certainly! Heavens, contrary to what some people in the back of the room believe, I look at everything with an open mind before I vote no.

On his popularity with male voters, and lack of it with women, Reagan responded:

The polls say I am doing all right with the men but I am way, way down with the women. Now maybe I am missing something, and you gals can help me. They say the women like Ronnie Ree-gin's charm. Now if you girls can give me a few tips, it would really help.

Immediately after asking the California legislature for a record $946 million tax increase, Governor Reagan had to leave for New York. Noting his good fortune, Reagan commented:

Pretty good timing. I'll drop the tax message and run.

—1967

I sometimes wonder what the Ten Commandments would have looked like if Moses had to run them through a Democratic legislature.

—1969

The credibility gap is so great in Washington they told us the truth the other day hoping we wouldn't believe it.

—1969

Reagan characterized his troubles with the Democrats to a gathering of state Republicans:

As you can well imagine, my mind has been turning back to that first time we met under these same circumstances four years ago. Then we were in the first month of a brand-new administration. Now it is the first month of a second term and we are all a little older, a little wiser—and still a few votes short in the legislature.

I think, regardless of who the [presidential] candidate is on the Democratic side, we [Republicans] have to take them very seriously, because we are a minority party, we're outnumbered. Having been a Democrat for a great part of my life—until I progressed and learned more—I know how difficult it is to get someone to leave his party and vote the other ticket. So I always run a little scared.

—JULY 14, 1972

When Reagan had to leave the state briefly, he left a note for his lieutenant governor, Robert Finch:

Dear Bob:

　　Solve something.

　　　　　　　　　　　　　　　　　　　　　　　　　Ron

P.S. Solve anything.

As a gubernatorial candidate, Reagan had once said that his feet were set in cement when it came to raising taxes. Once he became governor though, Reagan realized that he would have to raise taxes after all. As he told reporters:

　　Ladies and gentlemen, the sound you hear is the concrete beginning to crack around my feet.

At a Republican fund-raiser, Reagan commented:

　　We've heard a great deal about Republican fat cats—how the Republicans are the party of big contributions. I've never been able to understand why a Republican contributor is a fat cat and a Democratic contributor of the same amount of money is a public-spirited philanthropist.

　　　　　　　　　　　　　　　　　　　—LOS ANGELES, CALIFORNIA

　　　　　　　　　　　　　　　　　　　AUGUST 4, 1974

The Republican party is more in tune with the thinking of the majority of the American people than is the other major party or either of the splinter parties that started up. I do not believe that for vote-getting purposes you go out and vitiate, water down your true philosophical beliefs in order to persuade someone to vote for you. The Democrats have been doing things like that for years and that's why they have got a weird coalition that can't enjoy itself in one room together.

—NOVEMBER 12, 1974

Reagan told this story in a speech:

If I have dwelt overlong on troubles besetting all of us before getting to those peculiar to California and California's government, it was to guard against the experience of a gentleman who departed this earth from a point somewhere in western Pennsylvania. Arriving at the Pearly Gates he was greeted by Saint Peter and given an indoctrination course, during which he learned the heavenly old-timers had a story-telling ring and were particularly interested in newcomers who might have interesting earthly experiences to relate. He told Saint Peter he was a cinch to go over big—he was the sole survivor in his town of the Johnstown flood. Peter took him over to the group and gave him a flattering introduction and buildup. The Pennsylvanian stepped forward to begin his exciting story. At which point, Peter murmured in his ear: "By the way, that old guy in the front row is a fellow named Noah."

—New York, New York
January 17, 1968

Governments tend not to solve problems, only to re-arrange them.

Reagan said in a speech:

From those first few years when I kept you posted on how much we were saving on typewriter ribbons, these meetings have come to be an opportunity for me to report on the state of the state.

It is a pleasure to do so, especially this year because our fiscal situation is considerably improved and so are a few other things.

For example, last year when we met, the legislature was still in session. This year, they are still in session, but they have gone home for a while. The script is like one of those long-running soap operas on daytime TV.

Will Laura give up Mickey for Bill?

Will Bill find happiness with Cynthia?

Will there be action on tax reform and school finance?

Will they protect the environment without declaring the state off limits to people?

Will they ever start going home again on June 30?

Tune in next November.

—SACRAMENTO, CALIFORNIA
SEPTEMBER 8, 1972

Referring to the state's financial problems that he inherited when he became governor, Reagan said:

I didn't know whether I'd been elected governor or appointed receiver.

—MARCH 31, 1976

ON FOREIGN AFFAIRS AND FOREIGN POLICY

Of the nation's then current entanglement in the war in Vietnam, Reagan declared:

We could pave the whole country and put parking stripes on it and still be home for Christmas.

When asked by a reporter what he would have done in re-sponse to North Korea's seizure of the USS Pueblo, Governor Reagan replied:

I don't command any ships. California doesn't have a navy.

On war:

To blame the military for war makes about as much sense as suggesting that we get rid of cancer by getting rid of doctors.

—UNIVERSITY OF CALIFORNIA,
LOS ANGELES, JUNE 7, 1970

Reagan questioned America's motivation in Vietnam:

Somehow we are unable or at least unwilling to bring to terms, or force to an armistice, a ramshackle water-buffalo economy with a gross national budget hardly equal to that of Pascagoula, Mississippi.

After being questioned about his opinions on Vietnam and other international affairs, Reagan responded:

You know California doesn't have a foreign policy.

—1968

When his daughter Maureen reported that she had been to South Vietnam with a performance troupe and thought that a military victory was not possible, Reagan commented:

Well, now, while I'm partial to my daughter and love her very much, I don't think foreign policy should be decided by USO entertainers.

ON TAXES AND THE ECONOMY

Reagan's views on taxes:

The taxpayer, that's someone who works for the federal government but doesn't have to take a civil service examination.

—1968

On the value of the dollar:

Do you remember back in the days when you thought that nothing could replace the dollar. Today it practically has!

In a speech delivered in London, Reagan left no doubt about whether he preferred the private sector or government as an agent of economic improvement:

In my country some twenty-five years ago, you could make a long-distance call on a privately owned telephone system from San Francisco to New York for twenty-eight dollars. For that same amount of money, you could send 1,376 letters. Today, you can make the same telephone call for two dollars and a half and for that amount you can only send 41 letters. So the government is investigating the Bell system!

—LONDON, ENGLAND
FEBRUARY 2, 1970

Regarding that tax increase—I feel like the mother spanking her lovable but recalcitrant child—it hurt me more than it hurt you.

—MARCH 6, 1968

A Senate committee set up a distinguished research team, headed by a prestigious professor, who discovered that if you cut bus fares in half, more people would ride the bus. They got so excited about their discovery, they pursued it and learned you can further increase patronage if you pay people a dime to ride the bus. And even more people will ride if you pay them twenty cents. But then they had to report failure. They discovered that even when you pay people, you cannot get 100 percent use of rapid transit. This is my kind of sneaky way of telling that sixty million Americans still drive to work each day and we will be supporting new highways for years to come.

—SEPTEMBER 8, 1972

ON DOMESTIC AND SOCIAL ISSUES

Speaking to a group of middle-aged labor leaders, Reagan said:

You youngsters probably don't remember, but when I was young, golf was a sissy, rich man's game. So were boating and skiing and horseback riding. Today they're weekend sports for the working man; he doesn't have to go to Labor Day picnics.

—LABOR DAY, 1970

To another group of workers, Reagan sounded a note of empathy:

I'm just a citizen temporarily in public service.

—1970

Reagan said in a speech to the California State Bar Association:

Why does a criminal defendant with a clever lawyer seem able to run circles around some of our finest prosecutors with a seemingly bottomless barrel of time-consuming tricks? The public is frustrated and fed up with the sort of behavior that some defendants—and, indeed, some of their lawyers—are seemingly able to get away with in courtrooms, behavior that would not be tolerated in any kindergarten.

—Los Angeles, California
September 20, 1970

The crime problem has indeed become a matter of widespread concern, even among people of different philosophies. Today's hard-liner on law and order is yesterday's liberal who was mugged last night.

—August 1, 1973

On the voting age:

If we gave the vote to eighteen-year-olds, the next President of the United States will have three things to worry about: Vietnam, inflation, and acne.

—Sacramento, California
September 4, 1970

Rising drug use was one of the burning issues of the 1960s, and Governor Reagan was often confronted with the question of what to do about it. On one occasion, he responded as follows:

Let me get on the bandwagon with a counterpoint to the young pot smoker's plea or plaint. In New York recently at a dinner party a prominent editor sought the advice of several of us on "What do you tell a teenager who uses pot?" I suspect he was really asking "What do I do about my son?" I volunteered a few logical approaches, all of which he rejected. Finally (a little short of temper) I said, "Why don't you tell him if you catch him with one of those things in his mouth you'll kick his bottom side up between his shoulders?" Of course, he rejected that too.

In response to a constituent's letter about women's liberation, Reagan wrote:

I have read your letter . . . with great interest.

I am pleased to tell you I share your views about women's liberation. At the same time, I have to say I'm greatly pleased with the twenty-three ribs that have been assigned to me under the marital customs of our society. While I feel no need personally for the proposal you make to restore the equity in the matter of the missing rib, I have asked my legal advisers to look into all the ramifications of such a change in the law.

However, and above all, I want to thank you from the

bottom of my heart for your letter. Your complaint about the missing rib is the only thing I haven't been blamed for since I've been in this damn job.

On the "flower children" of the late 1960s:

Their signs said make love, not war, but they didn't look like they could do either.

—1969

Reagan also had the following sentiments for antiwar protesters:

Those young people [demand] the right to send blood to the enemy in Vietnam. I think they should be allowed to do that—providing they send it in the original container.

In response to advice offered by Washington Governor Daniel Evans on how to deal with college students, Reagan wrote:

Dear Dan,

Thanks so much for the brochure; I agree you have a right to be proud.

How would you feel about an exchange program with a choice selection from our Berkeley campus?

> Best regards,
> Ron
>
> —1967

Commenting on the exploitation of California's resources by other states, Reagan said:

The symbol of our state flag is a golden bear. It is not a cow to be milked.

On the social and political activists of the 1960s and '70s, Reagan attacked the inconsistencies of their positions:

The self-proclaimed revolutionaries and their legal champions denounce the "system" . . . yet they wrap themselves in the Constitution at every step in legal proceedings that involve them. To accept their idea of "justice" is to accept tyranny and anarchy. If Moses himself stood on Nob Hill [in San Francisco] and solemnly intoned the Ten Commandments, he probably would be denounced as a reactionary seeking to impose a repressive and outmoded life-style on the multitude.

—DECEMBER 2, 1971

If California's problems and California's people were put in a ring together, it would have to be declared a mismatch.

—1971

Hysterical pollution leads to political pollution with the result that all too often little or nothing gets done about actual pollution.

When Reagan learned that the Texas Senate voted on a resolution of praise for farm worker organizer Cesar Chavez, he wrote:

It makes me realize how true is the old saying, "No man's life or property is safe when the legislature is in session."

Cesar Chavez's terror tactics easily match those of the old-time night riders in the South. Incidentally, he's the one man I've ever known who can go on a fast and gain weight.

During a college demonstration when students chanted around the governor's limousine, "We are the future," Reagan scribbled a reply on a piece of paper, which he held up to the car window:

I'll sell my bonds.

When a young man suggested that the governor would establish better relations with the younger generation if he rode a motorcycle, Reagan respectfully declined:

I . . . think I'll have to stick to horseback riding. You see, there is the matter of security. When I go anyplace, I'm one of a group. We might look like Hell's Angels with all of us out there on motorcycles.

I had a nightmare last night; I dreamed I owned a Laundromat in Berkeley.

—1970

Reagan spotted a link between environmental problems and crime in his state:

I've got a new way to stop smog. Stop burning down schools.

—LABOR DAY, 1970

The young people want three political parties—one in power, one out of power, and one marching on Sacramento.

—LABOR DAY, 1970

After being briefed about California's vast and complex water system, Reagan joked:

I guess there's more to it than lying down by the creek and drinking your belly full.

Reagan on Bobby Kennedy:

Bobby Kennedy is so concerned about poverty because he didn't have any as a kid.

—1968

To set the record straight that he had never said, "If you've seen one redwood, you've seen them all," but rather had stated, "A tree is a tree. How many more do you have to look at?" Reagan told reporters:

Some of my best friends are redwoods.

I am opposed [to the legalization of marijuana]. And I am opposed because the score is not in yet [on the medical effects of its use]. The thing I think most people don't realize about legalization of marijuana is that fourteen companies have already registered trade names for marijuana cigarettes.

Once you make them legal, you're going to see billboards, and packs in the vending machines. Since marijuana is smoked for effect—not for the taste, as cigarettes—how are they going to advertise? What are they going to say—"Fly higher with ours"?

—BEFORE MEMBERS OF BOYS STATE
SACRAMENTO, CALIFORNIA
JUNE 22, 1972

During the Symbionese Liberation Army's rudimentary food distribution program, following the kidnapping of Patty Hearst, in California, the governor quipped:

It's too bad we can't have an epidemic of botulism.

—1974

ON THE PRESS

As photographers clicked away at the governor, they kept asking him to smile. Reagan responded:

If I keep on smiling, it looks like I have a very light-hearted speech.
Photographer: Will you gesture, Governor?
Reagan: I don't gesture very much when I talk.

The cameras kept snapping away, and finally Reagan said:

Now, you *will* get all these published?

—1967

At first, Reagan had told reporters that there would be no budget cuts for the University of California. When he changed his mind, the governor told reporters:

I goofed.

—JANUARY 17, 1968

To a reporter who wanted to know what Reagan had learned so far on the school finance problem, he said:

Not to answer your question.

—1971

And to another reporter who wanted to know if Reagan thought he would stay out of the 1976 presidential contest if Senator Edward Kennedy ran, Reagan retorted,

This is a great place to say, "No comment."

ON PERSONAL/FAMILY LIFE

When he returned to his home state of Illinois, Reagan said:

It is a homecoming for me and I could be very nostalgic. Of course when I lived here before, I was a Democrat and my whole family were Democrats. As a matter of fact, I had an uncle who lived here in Chicago who won a medal once for never having missed voting in an election for fifteen years . . . and he had been dead for fourteen.

—AUGUST 9, 1973

[Carving a turkey] was something I had to learn after I grew up, because when I was a kid we couldn't afford a turkey.

—NOVEMBER 14, 1973

When asked by a reporter to recall the nicest thing a girl ever did for him, the governor wrote:

The nicest thing a girl ever did for me was when a girl named Nancy married me and brought a warmth and joy to my life that has grown with each passing year.

I know she won't mind if I say the second nicest thing was a letter from a little fifth-grade girl last week. She added a P.S., "You devil, you." I've walked with a swagger ever since.

—1971

Reagan remarked to his secretary, Kathy Davis:

I have two favorite records for this music box. This one is "Silent Night." It's good for the office Christmas party. [The other one is] Mendelssohn's "Wedding March." Hmmmm, I wonder if I have the power to marry people. Could you get a legal ruling on that, Kathy?

Soon after Inauguration Day at the start of Reagan's first term, the governor's landlord sold the house to a group of Reagan's friends in order that they could rent it back to the Reagans, as the governor's mansion was a run-down firetrap. Reagan wrote to the landlord:

Knowing you receive unjustified complaints and undeserved criticism from miserable and unhappy tenants, and having a peculiar sympathy for anyone subject to that kind of treatment, I thought you might enjoy hearing from a happy tenant for a change.

My wife and I are very glad you bought out our previous landlord. (He should lose the money on the way to the bank.) Somehow, the place looks brighter already, possibly because we've painted a little here and there. (We won't knock out any walls, however, without letting you know.)

Anyway, the hot water is hot when it should be; the neighbors are quiet. (If they complain, they'll get a freeway right through their piazza.) The fuses don't blow, not even with all the lights on, and it's only ten minutes to my job.

Just changing landlords has my wife so revved up she is pushing furniture all over the place. (Frankly, it gives me a pain in the back.) But we want you to know we love you, we thank you heartily, and if keeping the place real nice will help show our appreciation, we'll do it. We don't even let the dog in the house, and the kids are severely limited. P.S.: I am talking to the people I work for about lowering your taxes.

—1967

The governor's mansion was situated near a well-trafficked street. Reagan more than once complained about the noise to his secretary, Kathy Davis:

Kathy, those damn trucks! I think they shift gears every time I begin falling asleep.

When a psychiatrist said publicly that Reagan's statements on California mental health care demonstrate that the governor was "under strain," Reagan responded:

Well, you know a head shrinker. He's probably sitting there right now looking at the pupils of my eyes on television. He can see me on a couch. Well, I want to tell you, if I get on a couch, it will be to take a nap.

When prodded by a reporter who wanted to know if Reagan actually had sold property he owned in Riverside County, California, Reagan replied:

Are you offering to buy, because I'm willing to sell?

Correspondence between John Wayne and Reagan:

Honorable Ronald Reagan
1341 45th Street
Sacramento, Calif.

Dear Ronnie:

Working like hell here at Fort Benning in the great state of Georgia.

The peaches have lost their fuzz, the frost is on the pumpkin, and we're working nights.

I read the enclosed article by Paul Harvey regarding your clear thinking and articulate manner in explaining same. It was refreshing to read something so aptly expressed. Thank God for Harvey, and keep up the good work, friend.

Love to Nancy.

Sincerely,
John Wayne

October 10, 1967

Mr. John Wayne
Camellia Motel
Columbus, Georgia

Dear Duke:

It was good to hear from you and thanks so much for sending the article. I'll keep it around as a chaser for some of those *Los Angeles Times* editorials.

I was in South Carolina last week, and if you hear a rumor that we're not well acquainted, I played down our friendship to get out of roping you into a benefit. Some people corralled me, had it all set up to fly you in and out of location in a Piper Cub I think, if I'd only get on the phone and urge you to do their benefit. I said I didn't think our relationship was close enough for me to do such a thing. I couldn't think of any other way of not calling you.

Nancy sends her love and I hope we'll be seeing you soon.

Best regards.

Sincerely,
Ronald Reagan
Governor

A letter to the San Francisco Chronicle *made some errors regarding his time in the Army. Referring to his autobiography, in which he discussed his military career, Reagan wrote back:*

One thing the letters have proven is that my book, *Where's the Rest of Me?* was not a best-seller. That's strange, too, because it is the best book I've ever written—it is also the only book I've ever written.

—1972

In a speech Reagan admitted:

I had never in my life thought of seeking or holding public office and I'm still not quite sure how it all happened.

—MARCH 31, 1976

In a speech to the National Sheriffs Association, Las Vegas, Governor Reagan said:

It's a pleasure to be here today—where the heat only comes from the sun.

Las Vegas is really a wonderful place. Where else outside of government do people throw money away? The big difference, of course, is that here you can do it yourself; in government, we do it for you.

But it's nice to see all you sheriffs out there. I've been a sheriff myself—you can't make a living in Hollywood for more than twenty-five years without being a sheriff, and if the picture makes money, polish the star, you'll wear it often.

—JUNE 19, 1967

Referring to his custom of keeping a bowl full of jelly beans in his office, Reagan once said:

Some political figures have endured in history as lions or conquerors or something equally impressive. It's a little frightening to think California history might record us as jelly beans.

You can tell a lot about a fella's character by whether he picks out all of one color or just grabs a handful.

Responding to a young man's comment that former actor, now Governor, Ronald Reagan makes a good good guy, "and a better bad guy," Reagan said:

Of course. You know it takes more acting to be a bad guy.

—FEBRUARY 3, 1967

Commenting on his newly acquired estate (the governor's mansion), Reagan observed:

I'm not one to look a gift house in the mouth.

—SACRAMENTO, CALIFORNIA
FEBRUARY 3, 1967

Reagan responded to the reporter who inquired if the governor would run for Vice President:

Before or after I fainted?

There is no shortage of energy with which we run the government of California, which we run on jelly beans!

—APRIL 26, 1974

While attending a board of regents meeting in California, university officials were discussing how the proposed Reagan cuts would harm the university. The governor, in response, drew a cartoon of Chicken Little carrying a mortar board on her head crying,

The sky is falling! The sky is falling!

—1967

If you want to know which way to go in the future, you have to know which path you took in the past and where you stepped in a gopher hole along the way.

—OCTOBER 15, 1974

There's something about football that no other game has. There's sort of a mystique about it. It's a game in which you can feel a clean hatred for your opponent.

—DECEMBER 19, 1971

Reagan told this football story:

I have an abiding love for the game. Maybe at this moment I should be drawing a parallel with someone else—a freshman at Notre Dame in the days of Knute Rockne. The squad was so big on opening day of football practice that Rock decided to thin it out in a rather primitive manner. He lined them up in two lines facing each other and put a soccer ball down between them. Then he explained that they would loosen up by trying to kick the ball over each other's goal line. And he made it clear that in the process a few shins might get kicked but football called for courage so that should not stop them. Then he looked down and the ball had disappeared. He said, "All right, where is it—who took the soccer ball?" The pint-sized freshman said, "Never mind the ball, Rock—when do we start kicking?"

—1971

Reagan said in his inauguration speech at the start of his second term:

Remembering our last meeting here under these same circumstances and in spite of the general belief that pain cannot be relived in memory, I recalled the cold of that day four years ago and decided that cold's ability to shrink and contract should be applied to my remarks. We will soon be indoors and thawed out!

I do not know whether time has a faster pace in Sacramento than elsewhere but these four years have gone by more swiftly than they did when I marked a four-year term as the period from freshman to senior. And yet in this four-year span we have plumbed the ocean depths and reached out to the stars. We have lived for extended periods on the ocean's floor and have walked on the surface of the moon. In fact, I have been up in the air a few times myself and once or twice have sought advice about living under water.

—1971

A Sacramento schoolteacher wrote to Reagan:

I thought you might enjoy a little humor today which happened in my kindergarten class.

I was briefing my class on the field trip we were to take the following day. One of the places scheduled to visit was the governor's mansion.

"Does anyone know who is the governor of California?" I asked.

(Complete silence)

"Oh, come now, children, you know his name. Ronald———?" (I hinted).

Instantly twenty-three hands shot up and twenty-three voices shouted triumphantly—

"RONALD MC DONALD!"

Reagan replied to the teacher:

I did get a kick out of it. I guess television has more power than any of us know.

I'll return the favor by telling you of the teacher who taught her class about magnets and their properties and then several weeks later gave a test and asked them what it was that was spelled with six letters, began with an *M,* and picked up things. Eighty-seven percent of the class said "mother." The true television anecdote, however, is the child who told her mother she liked her better than the other leading brands.

Thanks again, and please give my greetings to your class. Tell them I don't mind being Ronald McDonald at all.

Noticing that there was a large amount of official stationery remaining from the previous administration of Governor Pat Brown, Reagan asked his secretary, in the interest of fiscal responsibility:

Couldn't we just X out his name?

—1967

Mindful of the fact that the Democratic speaker of the California Assembly, Jesse Unruh, had gone from 285 to 200 pounds, Reagan commented:

It seems like it takes more than a tailor to change the image of Big Daddy.

Reagan once quipped:

I am very proud to be called a pig. It stands for pride, integrity, and guts.

—1970

We sure can't be like the fellow's wife who used to cut off both ends of the ham before she cooked it. When he asked her why she did that, she said because that's the way her mother always did it.

One day, he got the chance to ask his mother-in-law why she cut off both ends of the ham before she cooked it. And she said because that's the way her mother did it.

Came the holidays and Grandma was visiting and he told her about it and asked if that was true—why did she cut off both ends of the ham before she cooked it? She said, "That's simple. I never had a pan big enough to get the whole ham in it."

—MAY 31, 1974

CHAPTER 4

The Years in Between

In between his years as governor and President, Reagan took the time to examine his career and his future. He not only reflected on the changes facing the nation but also maintained his close relationship with the American people by speaking with citizens across the country. Throughout these transitional years, Reagan's sense of humor remained intact, and he continued to be known and loved for his charm.

Speaking of his days as an actor, Reagan commented:

In the business that I used to be in, you learn not to stay on stage too long. You learn there's a time you have to exit.

—EVANSVILLE, INDIANA
SEPTEMBER 24, 1978

When asked by a reporter whether he might run against Jimmy Carter for President in 1980, Reagan said that Carter remained "kind of a mystery" to him and that the former Georgia governor was a "hard target." He noted:

I've never seen anyone throw a peanut in the air and shoot it.

—EVANSVILLE, INDIANA
SEPTEMBER 24, 1978

On the fact that Republicans have never had much electoral appeal in times of economic stress:

For forty years or more this country has been following the lute song of the liberals. Suddenly, when they come undone with their planned economy, their deficit spending, and their deliberately planned inflation, which they said would maintain prosperity, how the hell do the conservatives get blamed?

Criticizing strict government controls on business, one of the major targets of the conservative philosophy of too much government, Reagan said:

We have all heard that if you build a better mousetrap, the world would beat a path to your door. Today if you build a better mousetrap, the government comes along with a better mouse.

—CULLMAN, ALABAMA
MARCH 21, 1975

Reagan was always pointing to the relationship between big government and the economy. Referring to the energy crisis of the mid-1970s, he said:

Our problem isn't a shortage of fuel, it's a surplus of government.

Having been a Democrat most of my life, I know how hard it is to mark that ballot the other way. It's almost like changing religions.

—1978

I don't have much faith in the third-party movement. I think a third party usually succeeds in electing the people they set out to oppose.

—Broadcast interview
San Francisco, California
August 29, 1975

Commenting on the victory of Democrat Jimmy Carter in 1976, Reagan said:

For the first time, the Democrats cannot fuzz up the issue by blaming the White House. They've got the whole enchilada now.

Politics is supposed to be the second oldest profession. I have come to realize that it bears a very close resemblance to the first.

—BUSINESS CONFERENCE

LOS ANGELES, CALIFORNIA

MARCH 2, 1977

On the Carter administration's foreign policy, most of which Reagan was diametrically opposed to, Reagan stated:

Internationally, they don't seem to know the difference between being a diplomat and a doormat. Take, for example, our approach to the . . . SALT talks, the refusal to acknowledge that the Soviet Union is building the greatest war machine known to man. Somehow, we've negotiated agreements [under which] we grow weaker and they grow stronger.

—LOS ANGELES, CALIFORNIA

DECEMBER 12, 1977

Reagan commented to a group of British exporters:

I was surprised you hadn't retaliated for some of the movies we sent you. But lately I've been listening to some of the records bought by our children and I think you're beginning to get even.

In my job these past eight years I've been a part of big-time education as a regent of the University of California—all nine campuses and more than 100,000 students. All I've seen since has convinced me if I had it to do over again, I'd still go to Eureka. Just being elbowed in a crowd as 27,000 students go milling between classes isn't necessarily where the action is.

Maybe the trouble with those professional women's lib-bers I mentioned earlier is related to something Will Rogers once said, "If women go on trying to be more and more equal to men, some day they won't know any more than men do."

—1976

CHAPTER 5

Reagan Looks
at Reagan

Everyone admires a person who can laugh at him or herself. The ability to admit error or defeat with a bit more than a smile is a quality that inspires leadership and respect. Ronald Reagan finds humor in just about everything, and much of it is self-effacing. Like his jovial observations about the world around him, Reagan's jokes directed at himself are both insightful and amusing.

There is no other way to better understand this fascinating and remarkable man than by reading what he has to say about himself. The anecdotes, witticisms, and stories in this chapter are drawn from all periods of Ronald Reagan's life and career.

I became the first Errol Flynn of the B's. I was as brave as Errol, but in a low-budget fashion.

—1965

As a candidate in the presidential primary race, Reagan complained to reporters that they were incorrectly fashioning his image.

The notion that [in my films] I never got the girl in the end [was incorrect]. In fact, I was usually the steady, sincere suitor—the one the girl finally turned to.

—1980

Commenting on his average acting career, Reagan said:

I'm no [Errol] Flynn or [Charles] Boyer. Mr. Norm is my alias.

When asked to autograph a picture from his film Bedtime for Bonzo, *which showed Ronald Reagan and the chimpanzee in bed together, Reagan wrote:*

I'm the one with the watch.

I have heard more than one psychiatrist say that we must imbibe our ideals from our mother's milk. Then, I must say, my breast feeding was the home of the brave baby and the free bosom. I was the hungriest person in the house but I only got chubby when I exercised in the crib; any time I wasn't gnawing on the bars, I was worrying with my thumb in my mouth—habits which have symbolically persisted throughout my life.

—1965

I love three things: drama, politics, and sports, and I'm not sure they always come in that order.

—1965

I was born in a small town in the Midwest, and I was in poverty before the rich folks got hold of it.

—1965

I'm not smart enough to lie.

—July 1980

I think I'm kind of moderate. Maybe we can overdo moderation.

—1980

Like almost every other young man, I had learned to drink—principally because it was against the law—and it was done out of a bottle that tasted like gasoline on the fraternity back porch or in a parked car.

Reagan has described himself as possessing a persistent naïveté throughout his lifetime. According to Reagan, he was often

unusually naive . . . blindly and busily joining every organization I could find that would guarantee to save the world . . . wide-eyed . . . light dawning in some obscure region in my head.

For a surgical procedure that drained excess blood that had collected on the surface of his skull, Reagan had to have a portion of his head shaved. He jokingly told his staff:

I guess my barber can have the week off.

—1989

In a letter to the editor of a college paper who claimed that Reagan had worn makeup at an appearance, he wrote:

Please tell Miss Marcus that I wore no makeup at the Commonwealth Club (I'm allergic to it). In the interest of press integrity also tell her she has a standing invitation to do a "white glove" test on my face the next time she is assigned to cover an appearance of mine!

The oldest President in United States history, Reagan often joked about his age. In a speech at London's fifteenth-century Guildhall, Reagan cracked:

It is comforting to be near anything that much older than myself. . . . Some even see my election to the presidency as America's attempt to show our European cousins that we too have a regard for antiquity.

Tip O'Neill once asked me how I keep myself looking so young for the cameras. I told him I have a good makeup team—the same people who've been repairing the Statue of Liberty.

—WASHINGTON, D.C.
MAY 15, 1986

At a White House dinner, Reagan told reporters:

I can remember when a hot story broke and the reporters would run in yelling, "Stop the chisels."

At a Gridiron Club banquet, Reagan told the crowd:

I heard one presidential candidate say that what this country needed was a President for the '90s. I was set to run again. I thought he said a President in his 90s.

Reagan kidded at the thirty-fifth annual Al Smith Dinner, commemorating the former Democratic governor of New York (1919–1928) and candidate in the 1928 presidential election:

There is no foundation to the rumor that I am the only one here who was at the original Al Smith Dinner.

During a televised Republican debate for the 1980 presidential nomination, Reagan remarked that wage and price controls had continually failed since the time of the Roman emperor Diocletian. He added:

I'm the only one here old enough to remember.

—1980

When the famous San Francisco attorney Jake Ehrlich asked Governor Reagan to autograph a picture of the two of them taken some twenty years earlier, Reagan wrote back:

I have just received your photograph, and am certain it is a fake. We were never that young.

In his 1992 Republican National Convention speech, Reagan joked:

Tonight is a very special night for me. Of course, at my age, every night's a very special night.

—HOUSTON, TEXAS

When Newsweek *reported that Reagan wore Pan-Cake makeup, Reagan denied it in a letter to the editor in which he said he never wore it offstage or onstage:*

You see, when I was younger, I could get along without it. And now it wouldn't help any.

—1966

Holding out a glass of tonic water, Reagan demonstrated his youthfulness, noting:

I feel just fine. Look, not even a ripple.

—1979

Quoting Thomas Jefferson's advice not to worry about age, Reagan quipped at a Washington Press Club dinner:

Ever since he told me that, I stopped worrying.

—1981

When I go in for a physical, they no longer ask how old I am. They just carbon-date me.

At a Republican National Convention, Reagan joked:

According to the experts, I have exceeded my life expectancy by quite a few years. Now this is a source of great annoyance to some, especially those in the Democratic party.

—HOUSTON, TEXAS
1992

Reagan was seventy-three when he ran for his second term as President. He responded to a query about this fact:

I believe Moses was eighty when God first commissioned him for public service.

—DIXON, ILLINOIS
FEBRUARY 6, 1984

In a speech three days after an operation to remove cancer cells from the tip of his nose, Reagan opened with the comment:

I know you're all admiring my suntan. You too can look like this—just sit out in the sun as long as I did.

Apologizing to some aides for being late, Reagan said:

The only reason I'm late, is that I had to oil my face.

—FEBRUARY 1981

I don't think it [age] is important. Samuel Colt invented the revolver when he was twenty, and Verdi wrote *Falstaff* when he was eighty. I'm somewhere in between. There are days when the legislature is especially busy and I feel older than Verdi—and days when I felt like Colt.

—AUGUST 22, 1972

There are those who will say having me here as speaker is a perfect job of typecasting. You are staging a celebration in the style and atmosphere of the last century. Some people would go even farther where I'm concerned and suggest that I belong to the Ice Age.

—COLUMBUS, GEORGIA
JULY 4, 1968

I was a near-hopeless hemophiliac liberal.

As the President-elect, Reagan reflected:

I remember some of my own views when I was quite young. For heaven's sake, I was even a Democrat.

—1980

While visiting a construction site, Reagan told workers that the hard hat they offered him would not fit because:

I have a pinhead.

—OCTOBER 1980

At a Gridiron Club dinner, Reagan joked:

It's true hard work never killed anybody, but I figure why take the chance.

—1989

CHAPTER 6

The Campaign for President, 1976

Although he came close, Reagan lost the Republican nomination for President in 1976 to Gerald Ford. But the long months of campaigning only served to fuel his wit. Reagan found much to laugh at in the world and, especially during the campaign, many of his jokes poked fun at the federal government. Had the government been his opponent for the nomination, he certainly would have won.

The government in Washington is spending some $7 million every minute I talk to you. There's no connection between my talking and their spending, and if they'll stop spending, I'll stop talking.

—MAY 1976

If you would render all the fat in government, you'd have enough soap to wash the world.

—JANUARY 1975

Bureaucrats favor cutting red tape—lengthwise.

—NOVEMBER 1975

About the paper generated by the federal bureaucracy, Reagan observed:

Wouldn't it make a great annual bonfire?

—FEBRUARY 1976

Reagan was firmly opposed to government handouts to business:

This is feeding the crocodile in hopes he will eat you last, but eat you he will.

When asked whether he thought the presidency should be limited to a single term, Reagan remarked:

There has been talk about a single-year sentence—er, term. . . . You can see I have no illusions about the job.

It's been said that if you put [President] Ford and me together in a dark room, you can't tell us apart philosophically. Well, if you turn on the light, you can.

As Reagan's reputation as the new champion of the conservative movement grew, he was increasingly compared with Barry Goldwater. On one occasion, Reagan responded:

Barry tried to tell us a number of things that a number of years ago we weren't quite ready to hear. He was perhaps a little ahead of his time. He was John the Baptist. There had to be a Barry Goldwater.

Quoting Bismarck, Reagan quipped:

If you like laws and sausages, you should never watch either one being made.

—OKLAHOMA CITY, OKLAHOMA
JUNE 4, 1976

Defending the vice-presidential candidate in 1976, Reagan said of Senator Richard Schweiker:

[He] has not become a captive of what I call the Washington buddy system.

—JULY 1976

Professional politicians like to talk about the value of experience in government. Nuts! The only experience you gain in politics is how to be political.

Reagan opposed busing schoolchildren, but he did support another kind of busing:

Busing some of the bureaucrats in Washington out into the country to meet the real people.

Any candidate who says he isn't frightened is a liar or a fool.

After having been asked about his position on the Panama Canal for the umpteenth time, Reagan kidded:

If they don't watch out, I'll come out and start defending the Erie Canal.

Reagan remarked that there has been only one benefit of detente for the United States.

Acquisition of the right to sell Pepsi-Cola in Siberia.
—FEBRUARY 1976

Referring to changes in state welfare programs, Reagan said:

If a state is mismanaged, you can move elsewhere.

I think we have two groups of [environmental] extremists. There are, of course, those people on one side who would pave the country over in the name of progress. There is an extremist group on the other extreme that wouldn't let you build a house unless it looked like a bird's nest. Now, I think there has to be a commonsense in-between that recognizes that people are ecology, too.

—AUGUST 1976

As Reagan's prospects grew, so did the number and difficulty of the questions posed to him by reporters. He commented:

Where before they were just nibbling around the edges, they come in biting now.

—JANUARY 1976

CHAPTER 7

The Campaign for
President, 1980

The 1980 campaign provided even more material for Reagan's characteristic jokes. Throughout the campaign and the general elections, Reagan took full advantage of the chance to reveal just how charming and amusing he could be. He kept his audiences laughing as he poked fun at the Democrats. One by one, he defeated his fellow contenders for the Republican nomination and then, captivating the American people, went on to win the presidential election, defeating Jimmy Carter.

As the campaign heated up, Reagan made many assaults

on Jimmy Carter's leadership in particular, often characterizing him as inept and lacking in vision. (But neither did he spare Walter Mondale or third-party candidate John Anderson—or indeed his own Vice President-to-be George Bush, whom he defeated in the primaries.)

ON BIG GOVERNMENT

In place of imagination, Mr. Carter calls for more government regulation. In place of ingenuity, he calls for more federal guidelines.

—SUNNYVALE, CALIFORNIA
SEPTEMBER 25, 1980

Talking to farmers, Reagan said:

If government payments were made on the basis of damage done by government, farmers all over America would be collecting disaster payments.

—NEVADA, IOWA
SEPTEMBER 29, 1980

After lamenting the 58 percent increase in government spending during the Carter administration, Reagan asked:

How many of you were able to increase your spending by 58 percent in the last four years? Well, that's how much government spending has gone up.

—Houston, Texas
October 29, 1980

After complaining about the mountains of undesired forms sent to citizens by the government, Reagan noticed photographers firing off picture after picture of him rolling an orange. He said of the fruit:

You could send them out instead of forms.

ON JIMMY CARTER AND OTHER OPPONENTS

I haven't had Jimmy Carter's experience. I wouldn't be caught dead with it.

—1980

When President Carter and Ronald Reagan were both campaigning in Columbus, Ohio, on the same day, Reagan told his supporters:

I heard some people are having trouble telling which motorcade is which. Well, his turns left at every corner.

—COLUMBUS, OHIO
1980

Reagan told supporters that he promised tax "increases" when he meant to say "decreases." He explained:

I've been talking about Carter so long that I make mistakes like he does.

—GRAND RAPIDS, MICHIGAN
NOVEMBER 1, 1980

When his microphone began to fail once, Reagan said:

Why do I have the feeling that I'm fading out? [Vice President] Mondale isn't in the city by any chance, is he?

—CHICAGO, ILLINOIS
OCTOBER 31, 1980

Asked how he thought he fared after the debate with President Carter, Reagan replied:

It seemed to go all right. I've examined myself and I can't find any wounds.

—November 1980

An Annapolis graduate may be at the helm of the ship of state, but it has no rudder.

Reagan confided to an aide about rival George Bush:

I never feel comfortable around him. Whenever he talks to me, he seems to be staring at my necktie.

When asked about Carter's accusation that Reagan was a "traveling salesman" for the American Medical Association, he commented:

Well, that's better than what he's been peddling.

I think Carter is very vulnerable on his record. To hear him talk about energy and inflation, you'd think someone else had been in charge the last three years.

[Carter had failed because of] his total inability to fill Jerry Ford's shoes.

—GRAND RAPIDS, MICHIGAN
NOVEMBER 1, 1980

My opponent would have you believe that instead of campaigning, I have been out starting nuclear wars.

—ST. LOUIS, MISSOURI
1980

After President Carter changed his campaign tactics, and made the campaign issues the primary focus, Reagan said:

I'm glad to see he's going to straighten up and fly right.

When asked whether he thought Carter had provided an ade-quate explanation for his brother Billy's actions regarding Libya, Reagan said:

Well, he does seem to be dragging his feet.

—PITTSBURGH, PENNSYLVANIA

1980

I had a dream the other night. I dreamed that Jimmy Carter came to me and asked why I wanted his job. I told him I didn't want his job. I want to be President.

—DETROIT, MICHIGAN

JULY 14, 1980

Carter was supposed to go on *60 Minutes* to talk about his accomplishments, but that left him with 59 minutes to fill.

—MIDDLEBURG, VIRGINIA

SEPTEMBER 13, 1980

Jimmy Carter's in the White House. Amy's in the tree-house. Billy's in the doghouse.

—TOPEKA, KANSAS

OCTOBER 20, 1980

Reagan gave this explanation of why Carter would not join the debate between him and John Anderson:

President Carter has been debating candidate Carter for the past three and a half years—and losing.

—HOUSTON, TEXAS
SEPTEMBER 16, 1980

After a prominent member of Carter's staff was accused of using marijuana, Reagan had this to say:

The President had ordered there be no hard liquor in the White House. And now we find some of the White House has been smoking pot. This is the first administration we can honestly say is high and dry.

—TOPEKA, KANSAS
OCTOBER 29, 1980

Reagan remarked about Carter:

Hell, I could have campaigned on the same things he campaigned on. The only difference was he forgot them between Plains and Washington.

—1980

When Reagan told a crowd of supporters that the litany of Carter's economic excuses "makes you wonder who's been in charge for the last three and a half years," his audience shouted back, "Amy! Amy!"—a reference to the President's remark that his daughter had told him that nuclear proliferation was the uppermost issue on her mind. Reagan then added:

That could be. I know he touched our hearts, all of us, the other night. I remember when Patti and Ron were little tiny kids we used to talk about nuclear power.

—MILWAUKEE, WISCONSIN
OCTOBER 1980

Reagan attacked President Carter's unwillingness to debate the most basic issues facing the country.

[Carter has] taken refuge behind a dictionary.

—1980

The conduct of the presidency under Mr. Carter has become a tragic comedy of errors. In place of competence, he has given us ineptitude. Instead of steadiness, we have gotten vacillation. While America looks for confidence, he gives us fear. His multitude of promises so richly pledged in 1976 have fallen by the wayside in the shambles of this administration.

—TEXARKANA, ARKANSAS
OCTOBER 29, 1980

No one should feel any obligation to reward his four years of total mismanagement with four more years to do the very same. He did not give us a government as good as the people, as he said he would do. He only gave us a government as good as Jimmy Carter, and that isn't good enough.

—NEW ORLEANS, LOUISIANA
OCTOBER 29, 1980

When I look at what [Carter] has done in the past four years, you can see why he spent so little time last night in the debate talking about his record. He has grown fond of referring to Franklin Roosevelt, Harry Truman, and John Kennedy. There's one Democratic President he doesn't talk about, and that's Jimmy Carter. To hear him talk, you would think someone else had been in charge for the last four years.

—HOUSTON, TEXAS
OCTOBER 29, 1980

When told that in a poll Congressman John Anderson had out-pointed him on their nationally televised debate, Reagan commented:

How come I still feel so good?

—PENSACOLA, FLORIDA
SEPTEMBER 23, 1980

On Carter's statement "I will never lie to you":

After hearing that line about twenty times I was reminded of Ralph Waldo Emerson's line, "The louder he
talked of his honor, the faster we counted our spoons."

—JACKSONVILLE, FLORIDA
SEPTEMBER, 4, 1980

I've been very busy, as you know, starting nuclear
wars and doing away with social security and all those
things—that is, if you listen to what the other fellas are
saying.

—1980

No matter how much [Carter] tries to run away
from his record, he has to account for it to the American
people.

—DES PLAINES, ILLINOIS
OCTOBER 31, 1980

*In response to Carter's charges that Reagan was out to destroy
America and the world, Reagan quipped:*

You know, after you've canceled social security and
started the war, what else is there for you to do?

During a debate with President Carter, Reagan said:

I know the President's supposed to be replying to me, but sometimes I have a hard time in connecting what he's saying with what I have said my positions are. I sometimes think he's like the witch doctor that gets mad when a good doctor comes along with a cure that'll work.

—OCTOBER 1980

The President said I'm irresponsible. Well, I'll admit to being irresponsible if he'll admit to being responsible [for some of the nation's problems].

During their debate, Reagan asked his opponent, John Anderson:

John, would you *really* find Teddy Kennedy preferable to me?

On Government and Politics in General

In response to finding out that he had been endorsed by staunch liberal Eugene McCarthy, Reagan said:

Maybe this will give some people confidence that I don't eat my young.

—1980

In a remark to his fellow westerners, Reagan quipped:

Let's turn the sagebrush rebellion into a sagebrush solution.

—GRAND JUNCTION, COLORADO
SEPTEMBER 23, 1980

After his overwhelming victory in the South Carolina primary, Reagan told reporters:

I have been telling some of you that I'm cautiously optimistic. Now I'm cautiously ecstatic.

After his victory in the New Hampshire primary, Reagan told the press:

You fellas are going to call me whatever you want to call me, but I have a hunch it's going to be "front-runner."

When a reporter asked if Reagan had watched the Roger Mudd interview with Senator Ted Kennedy, he replied:

Nancy and I were so tired last night, we watched from bed and fell asleep.

Reagan invented his own Eleventh Commandment:

Thou shalt not criticize other Republicans.

And, later a Twelfth:

Thou shalt not be overconfident.

—JULY 1980

Reagan lamented Carter's relations with Congress:

Pennsylvania Avenue must be a two-way street.

—WASHINGTON, D.C.

SEPTEMBER 15, 1980

When someone shouted, "I want Teddy," at a Reagan rally, Reagan quipped:

There's a fella back there who wants Teddy—he's sick.

—SAN DIEGO, CALIFORNIA

JUNE 2, 1980

Referring to easterners' impressions of him, Reagan said:

Horns begin to grow as soon as I cross the Mississippi.

—APRIL 1980

When disrupted by hecklers, Reagan said:

At some point back there, those who deny the rights of others to speak who don't share their particular views were raising their hands in a salute more familiar in my younger days. They were saying, "Heil, Reagan." Well you know, I take a little pride, if you'll pardon me, in the fact that if it wasn't for my generation, they'd be saying, "Heil, some-body," today.

—HUNTINGTON BEACH, CALIFORNIA
OCTOBER 13, 1980

Speaking to Democrats, Reagan said:

I know what it's like to pull the Republican lever for the first time, because I used to be a Democrat myself, and I can tell you it only hurts for a minute and then it feels just great.

—BAYONNE, NEW JERSEY
OCTOBER 25, 1980

It isn't always necessary to make [legislators] see the light, as long as you can make them feel the heat.

—1980

Reagan was asked by a reporter to comment on a remark by pollster Lou Harris, who said that because Reagan had done well in the debate with President Carter, the election was now Reagan's to lose:

Well, I'll tell you that if Lou Harris says the election is mine to lose, the best thing for me to do is stop talking to you people.

He then grinned and added:

I'm only kidding.

—New Orleans, Louisiana
October 29, 1980

During a debate with President Carter, Reagan remarked:

But when I quoted a Democratic President, as the President says, I was a Democrat. I said many foolish things back in those days.

—October 1980

On Foreign Affairs and Foreign Policy

In response to Panamanian claims to the Canal Zone, Reagan said:

We should tell Panama's tinhorn dictator just what he can do with his demands for sovereignty over the Canal Zone. We bought it, we paid for it, and they can't have it.

Commenting on President Carter's claims, Reagan said:

The President is determined to have me start a nuclear war. Well, I'm just as determined that I'm not going to.

—OCTOBER *10, 1980*

Alluding to Carter's troubles with his brother Billy and the Libyan government, Reagan pointed out that U.S. oil imports from this unstable country had increased, remarking:

Maybe he should send more relatives over there.

CLEVELAND, OHIO
SEPTEMBER 19, 1980

When reporters asked candidate Reagan to respond to President Carter's charge that Reagan proposed military solutions to various diplomatic problems, he said:

You fellows have heard about everything I've said. Have you ever heard me say that? I'll bet none of you ever have because I've never said it.

—PENSACOLA, FLORIDA
SEPTEMBER 23, 1980

Carter couldn't get the Russians to move out of Cuba so he's moving out the Cubans.

In response to Carter's accusations that Reagan was a warmonger, Reagan responded:

You know, in spite of what the President has said, I've never had my thumb on the button once.

—1980

Reagan said of President Carter's Middle East policy:

[It] zigzags and flip-flops in ever more rapid gyrations, trying to court favor with everyone.

—WASHINGTON, D.C.
SEPTEMBER 3, 1980

You know, now that I have a farm they send me the Sears catalog. And I must confess I'm impressed. There's such a wide variety of consumer products available through that one company; we ought to send every Russian a Sears catalog.

On Taxes and the Economy

When it was reported that President Carter forecast better economic times, Reagan retorted:

I don't know what country he was talking about.

—CLEVELAND, OHIO
MAY 30, 1980

Maybe it's about time we had a President who remembered the Great Depression and what it was all about.

—BIRMINGHAM, MICHIGAN
OCTOBER 16, 1980

Depression is when you're out of work. A recession is when your neighbor's out of work. Recovery is when Carter's out of work.

Yes, the mighty music of American economic progress has been all but silenced for four years of Mr. Carter's failures.

—OCTOBER 24, 1980

The next time you go to the supermarket and see that astronomical number on the little white piece of paper, just remember that Mr. Carter told you not to worry about fluctuations.

At a press conference Reagan charged President Carter with dissimulating:

[Carter] stood there with his bare face hanging out and said the inflation rate was going to stay in the single-digit level. How can it stay where it hasn't been and isn't now?

We now know what Mr. Carter plans to do with four more years. Catch your breath, hold on to your hats, and grab your wallets because Jimmy Carter's analysis of the economy means that his answer is higher taxes.

—LIMA, OHIO
OCTOBER 15, 1980

Commenting on the Carter administration's changing the statistical base of the producer price index, Reagan lamented:

Now measured by the way this administration has used the imperial incumbency over the past year, I am not surprised [by] the recent—forgive me for this—"Jimmying" of official government statistics. What we need is a change in the economy and not a change in the statistics.

—CHERRY HILL, NEW JERSEY

OCTOBER 6, 1980

Referring to Carter's economic policies, Reagan commented:

He said he'd do something about unemployment. He did. In April, 825,000 Americans lost their jobs.

—CLEVELAND, OHIO

MAY 30, 1980

We started with an administration that didn't have any plan, any economic plan, of what they were going to do with the presidency other than enjoy it. And now we're reaping this harvest, and I look forward to turning around some of the things that have gone wrong.

—CHICAGO, ILLINOIS

OCTOBER 30, 1980

[Carter will] continue to take us into the economic Dark Ages.

—LIMA, OHIO

OCTOBER 15, 1980

First we must overcome something the present administration has cooked up: a new and altogether indigestible economic stew, one part inflation, one part high unemployment, one part recession, one part runaway taxes, one part deficit spending and seasoned by an energy crisis. It's an economic stew that has turned the national stomach. It is as if Mr. Carter had set out to prove, once and for all, that economics is indeed a "dismal science."

—1980

Reagan called President Carter's economic plan:

Quicksilver economics.

—CHERRY HILL, NEW JERSEY
OCTOBER 6, 1980

Reagan quipped:

The current tax code is a daily mugging.

Asked by an Iowa farmer if he was concerned about rising farm-land prices, Reagan replied:

Not when I sell, but when I buy.

—SEPTEMBER 31, 1980

ON DOMESTIC AND SOCIAL ISSUES

You know, I think the best possible social program is a job.

—1980

On the Press

Reagan was spotted reading a New York Times *analysis of his latest foreign policy speech:*

I want to see what these bastards are saying so I can protect myself. You can sure tell when you're in hostile territory.

—1980

When bothered by hecklers, Reagan told his audience:

I hope my mike can outlast their bullhorns.

And when it did not, he showed his displeasure with their shouting and singing by commenting:

You know, they can't even sing.

—Claremont, California
October 13, 1980

On a campaign bus in snowy New Hampshire, Reagan kidded:

If anyone hears dogs barking, it's because the next leg will be done by sled.

*Because of hectic scheduling, Reagan appeared a little over-
dressed at a Virginia farmhouse:*

I'm sorry I'm not dressed the way I should be for a party
like this, but I have to run off to Washington—although I
counted on doing that more along January.

—MIDDLEBURG, VIRGINIA
SEPTEMBER 13, 1980

I am what I have always been, and I intend to remain
that way.

—NOVEMBER 1, 1980

When interrupted by a heckler once, Reagan responded:

Aw, shut up.

After his supporters cheered and applauded, Reagan went on:

My mother always told me I should never say that, but
I heard so many like him and this is the last day of the campaign and I thought for just once I could say it.

—SAN DIEGO, CALIFORNIA
NOVEMBER 3, 1980

Speaking in Los Angeles, Reagan joked:

Nancy and I have been so homesick, campaigning all over the East, that we would be happy to be here, even in the smog siege.

—OCTOBER 13, 1980

About his regular after-dinner speaking engagement (of which there were plenty), Reagan commented:

I'm saying the same things I've been saying for twenty-five years on the mashed-potato circuit. So is a preacher in church on Sunday.

CHAPTER 8

The Presidency

Ronald Reagan was not only the oldest President in our nation's history but also one of the most highly esteemed. He made the transition into office smoothly and soon became known as one of the most amiable, and certainly one of the funniest, Presidents the nation had ever known.

In a decade of unprecedented social and technological change, Reagan had his work as President cut out for him, but his lighthearted nature never failed to carry him through the difficult times. During the first one hundred days of his administration, Reagan's cleverness remained an energetic force behind his programs and proposals. His characteristic good humor during his two terms as President, 1981–1989, not only made him adored by many, but also provides us insight into this magnificent man and his view of the world.

ON INAUGURATION AND FIRST DAYS
IN OFFICE

Shortly before his first inauguration as President, Reagan was briefed by his advisers on the many problems facing America. He quipped:

I think I'll demand a recount!

When told that President Kennedy assessed the presidency this way, "The pay is pretty good and you can walk home to lunch," Reagan remarked:

Oh? I've been here two days and I've had lunch both days in this office.

—WASHINGTON, D.C.
JANUARY 22, 1981

*Soon after the inauguration festivities died down, and Ronald
Reagan settled into his role as President of the United States:*

Good morning all—a good morning without the Marine Band. It's getting very quiet down here.

—WASHINGTON, D.C.

JANUARY 23, 1981

*At the White House, Reagan said to the American hostages
freed from Iran and to their families:*

Now don't get worried. There's not going to be a
lengthy speech. I've been in office now for one week and
one of the things I've found out is that there are a few orders
that I can give. So tonight I am officially ordering that all of
you have a good rest, catch up with your families, and as
much as Nancy and George and I and Barbara enjoy having
you as our guests, we simply don't want to keep you from
the privacy that you now deserve.

*After meeting with Speaker of the House Thomas P. O'Neill,
Reagan told reporters:*

He said I was in the big leagues now.

After pausing a moment, the President added:

I gathered that already.

—WASHINGTON, D.C.

JANUARY 22, 1981

Commenting on his status of being newly elected, Reagan said:

I'm a prisoner of my schedule again.

Concerning his working conditions, Reagan pined:

I feel like a bird in a gilded cage.

During his first day in office, the President wondered if the previous administration had left anything for him. He soon found out, noting:

Well, they've left me some paper clips.

—WASHINGTON, D.C.

JANUARY 1981

Reagan noted at a ceremony for the swearing-in of presidential appointees:

Thank you very much. Please, I want you to know that I don't expect every morning to be greeted by the Marine Band.

—JANUARY 21, 1981

Reagan said at a gathering of members of the Cabinet and their families:

Good morning, all of you. I had thirty or forty minutes of speech but then I just thought, no, never mind. As you know, this was supposed to be a swearing-in but certain branches of the government don't operate as fast as the others, and so there won't be a swearing-in but we'll get the pictures taken. I'm surprised with some of the delay that some of you who are Cabinet members, and not yet sworn in in some of the sections we've had, haven't gotten up and said, I don't work here and walked out.

—WASHINGTON, D.C.
JANUARY 22, 1981

After his first day in office, the President said:

It's been a very wonderful day. I guess I can go back to California. Can't I?

—JANUARY 1981

Reagan soon realized how much work the presidency entailed. During one of his brief strolls outside the White House, he joked about being office-bound, saying:

This is outside, isn't it?

—WASHINGTON, D.C.
JANUARY 1981

Reagan quipped at one of his inaugural balls:

Hi. Ladies and gentlemen, we're delighted to be here. I know that it can be only for a few minutes because there are ten of these and we're going to get to all of them. And the fellows that are engineering getting us around say it's only going to take four and a half hours.

—WASHINGTON, D.C.
JANUARY 20, 1981

Reagan said before the crowd at one of his inaugural balls:

You look very pretty tonight [addressing Mrs. Reagan]. I think she looks gorgeous as a matter of fact. On the way over someone said when we got here, we might even have a minute or two to dance, but I don't think so. Well, they've

got us in public housing and we'll dance when we get the
heck there.

—WASHINGTON, D.C.

JANUARY 20, 1981

ON BIG GOVERNMENT

In a press conference on assistance to farmers, Reagan said:

The nine most terrifying words in the English language
are, "I'm from the government and I'm here to help."

—CHICAGO, ILLINOIS

AUGUST 2, 1986

Reagan on Congress and the federal budget:

Cures were developed for which there were no known
diseases.

—1981

*Reagan's view on what should be the role of government with
respect to the economy was acerbicly presented in the following
comment:*

[According to the Democrats,] government's view of
the economy could be summed up in a few short phrases. If

it moves, tax it. If it keeps moving, regulate it. And if it stops moving, subsidize it.

The President also felt that most other aspects of life should be free of government regulation and intervention. The primary function of government was to provide a defense for the nation and protect the rights of its citizens, especially its entrepreneurs.

Reagan on big government:

There's a clear cause and effect here that is as neat and predictable as a law of physics: as government expands, liberty contracts.

ON GOVERNMENT AND POLITICS IN GENERAL

Poking fun at Congress, Reagan once told journalists:

I've been criticized for going over the heads of Congress. . . . So what's the fuss? A lot of things go over their heads.

As President-elect, Reagan felt that it was important to meet as many members of Congress as possible. He later observed:

I've been smiling so much my jowls hurt.

—1980

In a speech before the White House News Association, Reagan joked with association president Ken Blaylock:

By the way, Ken . . . I understand you're the first president of this organization to serve a third consecutive term. . . . A third term? That's not a bad idea.

WASHINGTON, D.C.
MAY 15, 1986

At a luncheon for Republican senators and congressmen, the President-elect decided to keep his comments brief, remarking:

If I keep on with this, I'll be making a campaign speech, and I don't want to do that.

—1980

At a meeting with his Cabinet and overzealous budget director David Stockman, the group quickly approved a mere $125 mil-

lion reduction in Department of Energy administration costs.
Fearing Stockman would have more to cut, Reagan asked for
comments, and hearing none, immediately said:

Good! All right. Turn the page quick.

Reagan's view on politics:

There is no such thing as a left or right. There is only
an up or down.

At a human rights convention, Reagan said:

The other day, someone told me the difference between
a democracy and a people's democracy. It's the same difference between a jacket and a straitjacket.

—DECEMBER 10, 1986

Referring to the program to push his budget proposals through
Congress, Reagan said:

We may not run this like a quarter mile, but we'll run it.

—WASHINGTON, D.C.

JANUARY 1981

The best minds are not in government. If any were, business would hire them anyway.

When Governor James Thompson of Illinois warned the President that some of his colleagues would accept Reagan's budget cuts over their dead bodies, Reagan quipped:

Well, maybe over their dead bodies isn't a bad idea.

At a roast for White House adviser Lyn Nofziger, Reagan quipped:

I'm glad the Young Americans for Freedom is having a fund-raiser for Lyn. I hope he can now afford a new suit.

I also believe that we conservatives, if we mean to continue governing, must realize that it will not always be so easy to place the blame on the past for our national difficulties. You know, one day the great baseball manager Frankie Frisch sent a rookie out to play center field. The rookie promptly dropped the first fly ball that was hit to him. On the next play he let a grounder go between his feet and then threw the ball to the wrong base. Frankie stormed out of the dugout, took his glove away from him, and said, "I'll show you how to play this position." And the next batter slammed a line drive right over second base. Frankie came in on it, missed it completely, fell down when he tried to chase it, threw down his glove, and yelled at the rookie, "You've got center field so screwed up nobody can play it."

—WASHINGTON, D.C.
MARCH 20, 1981

When asked whether a certain program could be reduced even further, Reagan told a Cabinet secretary:

Go ahead and cut it. They're going to hang me in effigy anyway, and it doesn't matter how high.

Differences among his aides moved Reagan to observe:

Sometimes our right hand doesn't know what our far right hand is doing.

When asked whether the President had denied a federal appointment to a woman who publicly disagreed with his budget cuts, Reagan turned the question around on himself, asking:

How can you say that about a sweet fellow like me?

Regarding budget cuts, Reagan was asked, "Can you stand the political heat on this one?" He replied:

Look, I come from a warm climate . . . I can stand the heat.

At a Republican dinner party, Reagan said:

We're the party that wants to see an America in which people can still get rich.

—1982

When aides told Reagan he should give the speeches speechwriters had drafted for him, the President said:

No, I want to stick with mine.

Reagan on Congress:

Congress loves making hard deals that include tax hikes; just don't expect it to keep its side of the bargain.

—1982

On Foreign Affairs and Foreign Policy

Commenting on the fact that he had seen the movie Rambo *the night before the 1985 hijacking of an American plane, Reagan quipped:*

I'll know what to do next time.

In his first trip out of the White House after the bombing of Libya, Reagan told reporters:

These last few weeks have really been hectic . . . what with Libya, Nicaragua, the budget, taxes. I don't know about you, but I've been working long hours. I've really been burning the midday oil.

CBS's Gary Schuster and Reagan joked about the President's dog, Lucky, at a White House Correspondents Association dinner:

Gary Schuster: The President has called, as you know, Qaddafi a mad dog . . . and apparently he meant it. He's consid-

ered having Qaddafi flown to the Santa Barbara Ranch to
keep Lucky company.

Reagan: Gary, I think more of Lucky than that.

—APRIL 1986

*Aware of legal problems in his administration's secret dealings
with Iran for the release of American hostages, Reagan joked at
a White House meeting:*

Well, the American people will never forgive me if I
fail to get the hostages out over this legal problem. . . . But
the visiting hours [in jail] are Thursday.

—DECEMBER 7, 1985

*In response to a reporter's question of what he thought of Amer-
ican companies that wanted to resume doing business with Iran,
Reagan replied:*

My opinion of American companies that want to
resume business with Iran? I hope they're going to do it
by long distance. We wouldn't want to go back to having
just a different cast of characters but the same show
going on.

—WASHINGTON, D.C.
JANUARY 29, 1980

*Reagan's top aide told him, "We don't ever want to see a pic-
ture of you kissing [Soviet leader Leonid] Brezhnev," referring
to the ceremony in which President Carter kissed the Soviet
leader. Reagan replied:*

You won't even see me kissing Brezhnev's wife!

—WASHINGTON, D.C.

1981

*When a Soviet plane downed a South Korean airliner, Reagan
said in a radio address:*

The Soviet Union owes the world the fullest possible
explanation and apology for their inexcusable act of brutality.
So far they've flunked the test.

—1983

*Reagan commented on the seemingly slow pace of rebuilding after
the bombing of the United States embassy annex in Beirut:*

Anyone that's ever had their kitchen done over knows
that it never gets done as soon as you wish it would.

At an arms-control treaty signing ceremony with Soviet leader Mikhail Gorbachev, Reagan repeated a favorite saying of his, citing the wisdom of an old Russian maxim:

Trust, but verify.
Gorbachev then interrupted and said with a smile:
You repeat that at every meeting.
Reagan laughed along with reporters and then said:
I like it.
After producing another Russian proverb, Reagan noted:
I'm becoming quite an expert in Russian proverbs.

—1987

Reagan said of the new closeness between the Soviet Union and the United States that developed during his presidency:

I want the . . . closeness to continue. And it will, as long as we make it clear that we will continue to act in a certain way as long as they continue to act in a helpful manner. If and when they don't, at first pull your punches. If they persist, pull the plug.

—JANUARY 11, 1989

In his farewell speech from the Oval Office, Reagan reflected on his years in office; mentioning an economic conference, he said:

It was back in 1981, and I was attending my first big economic summit, which was held that year in Canada. The meeting place rotates among the member countries. The opening meeting was a formal dinner for the heads of government of the seven industrialized nations. Well, I sat there like the new kid in school and listened, and it was all François [Mitterrand] this and Helmut [Kohl] that. They dropped titles and spoke to one another on a first-name basis. Well, at one point I sort of leaned in and said, "My name's Ron."

ON TAXES AND THE ECONOMY

Joking about exports at a Washington Gridiron Club dinner, Reagan said:

I think we should keep the grain and export the farmers.
—MARCH 23, 1985

At a correspondents' dinner, Reagan announced that he and House Speaker Jim Wright agreed on something.

There are three things we must do to balance the trade deficit. We can't remember what they are.
—APRIL 1987

Of the graduated income tax, Reagan said:

The entire graduated income tax structure was created by Karl Marx.

Of the economy, Reagan said to a crowd:

But it's going to be a tough fight. There are those who would rather get theirs now than cure inflation. They're going to do everything they can to preserve the status quo. And I ask you, after two years of double-digit inflation and economic stagnation, do you really want to keep the status quo? [Shouts of no from the audience.]

I didn't think so. *Status quo,* you know, that is Latin for "the mess we're in."

—WASHINGTON, D.C.
MARCH 16, 1981

We can bring inflation down and we can get America building again. You know, if that sounds like we're asking for miracles, well, on this eve of St. Patrick's Day, someone with the name of Reagan, I think, is entitled to think in terms of miracles.

You know, there was a lad in court in New York

bandaged from his toes to his chin suing for $4 million as a result of an accident and he won the suit. The lawyers for the insurance company went over to him and they said, "You're never going to enjoy a penny of this. We're going to follow you twenty-four hours a day. We know you're faking and the first time you move, we'll have you." He said, "Will you now? Well," he said, "let me tell you what's going to happen to me. They're coming in here with a stretcher. They're taking me in a car—an ambulance. They're driving me straight to Kennedy Airport and they're putting me on the airplane in that stretcher. We're flying direct to Paris, France, and there they're taking me on the stretcher off the plane, putting me in another ambulance. We're going direct to the Shrine of Lourdes and there you're going to see the damnedest miracle you ever saw."

—MARCH 16, 1981

Republicans believe every day is the Fourth of July, but Democrats believe every day is April 15.

Reagan told his economic advisers:

I come from a warm climate. I enjoy a warm climate. I'll take a warm climate.

Reagan once quipped about the federal deficit:

I'm not worried about the deficit: it's big enough to take care of itself.

—1984

As Reagan said before the election of his successor, George Bush:

America's economy is a Grand Prix racer. The way to keep it on track is to give George Bush and Dan Quayle the checkered flag.

—1988

ON DOMESTIC AND SOCIAL ISSUES

Welfare's purpose should be to eliminate, as far as possible, the need for its own existence.

Reagan said at a dinner honoring Secretary of Agriculture John Block held by the National Association of State Departments of Agriculture:

But we've changed gears here and I tried to warn John about some of the things that—I remember when Ezra Taft Benson was secretary of agriculture, and he was out in the country and hearing reports from people in the farm areas and talking to them and at one place, there was a fellow that was giving him a really bad time, really complaining and Ezra turned around and looked at some notes that someone handed him and then turned back and said, "Now, wait a minute. You didn't have it so bad." He said, "You had twenty-six inches of rain last year." And the fellow says, "Yes, I remember the night it happened."

. . . I know once when I was out on the mashed potato circuit before I—that was when I was unemployed—I was speaking to a farm group in Las Vegas and on the way in to where I was to speak there was one of those fellows that was there for the action and he recognized me. And he said, "What are you doing here?" I told him. He said, "What are a bunch of farmers doing in Las Vegas?" And I just couldn't help it. I said, "Buster, they're in a business that makes a Las Vegas craps table look like a guaranteed annual income."

—WASHINGTON, D.C.
MARCH 17, 1981

When asked about a second term, Reagan commented:

Well, you know I never could have achieved welfare reform in California without a second term.

As Reagan said at a news conference:

It's difficult to believe that people are starving in this country because food isn't available.

—1986

Reagan once told the following story during a speech at a White House ceremony commemorating the Bicentennial Year of Air and Space Flight:

You know, I have to tell you a little personal experience here. I was governor of California back in the riotous days of the sixties. . . . I remember one day when a group of the leaders of that came from the campuses of the University of California to Sacramento. They had demanded a meeting with me. So, they came in . . . [and] one of them who was the spokesman said to me, "Governor, it's impossible for you to understand us." . . . I said, "Well, we know more about being young than you do about being old." And he said, "No, your generation cannot understand their own sons and daughters." He said, "You didn't grow up in an era of computers figuring in seconds what it used to take men years to figure out." . . .

Usually you only think of the answer after you're gone, but the Lord was good to me. And . . . I finally interrupted him, and I said, "Wait a minute. It's true what you said. We didn't grow up, my generation, with those things. We invented them."

—WASHINGTON, D.C.
FEBRUARY 7, 1983

ON THE PRESS

Having some fun with his audience of reporters, Reagan said:

I've got a news item for you . . . We have a spin-off from our "Star Wars" research. It's a helmet for me to wear at press conferences. All I do is push a button and it shoots down incoming questions.

—WHITE HOUSE CORRESPONDENTS ASSOCIATION DINNER
WASHINGTON, D.C.
APRIL 1987

At a press conference a reporter prefaced his question by saying, "Mr. President, I'd like to get back to El Salvador for a second." Reagan retorted:

Do we have to?

—WASHINGTON, D.C.
MARCH 6, 1981

Reagan loved to joke with the press. Poking fun at the television networks, Reagan said:

I understand that ABC's been having some budget problems. . . . The news division's already laid off three hair stylists.

And that sweater Dan Rather wears is really from Goodwill Industries.

And I hear that NBC's going to do a hard-hitting report saying the only reason Ron Reagan's career is taking off is because he has a famous father. The guy saying it will be Chris Wallace . . . the son of *60 Minutes* inquisitor Mike Wallace.

Reagan told reporters in the White House Correspondents Association:

Mark Twain is supposed to have said there's nothing harder to put up with than the annoyance of a good example, and you certainly have been that to the White House press corps.

—CAMP DAVID, MARYLAND
APRIL 25, 1981

Joking with ABC reporter Sam Donaldson, Reagan said:

At my last press conference I thought that gimmick of wearing a red dress to get my attention went a little too far. Nice try, Sam.

*Joking about news photographers' ordinarily casual appearance,
Reagan said at the 1986 White House News Photographers
Association dinner:*

I guess I'd better begin with an apology for being a little
late. I told the man at the hotel desk I was looking for a room
full of people in blue jeans.

—WASHINGTON, D.C.
MAY 15, 1986

I was taken to task in the press the other day for (saying)
lay-ison. And they thought that I just didn't know, but I'll
tell you, I'm guilty. The Army has some words of its own.
And when I was a reserve cavalry officer, the Army called it
lay-ison just like they call *oblique* oblike in the army. So now,
I'm a civilian so I'll call it liaison.

—WASHINGTON, D.C.
MARCH 16, 1981

*Joking at a White House News Photographers Association din-
ner, Reagan said:*

There isn't a person here who isn't willing to go to great
lengths to get a good shot . . . Just this afternoon I stepped outside
the Oval Office to feed the squirrels. Six photographers came
out of the bushes. It's okay. I had enough peanuts to go around.

—WASHINGTON, D.C.
MAY 15, 1986

Reagan kidded at a Washington Press Club

Thank you very much and thank you especially for not giving me a question. I'm surprised to find myself at this podium tonight. I know your organization was founded by six Washington newspaperwomen in 1919. It seems like only yesterday.

I know that it was Washington's National Press Club for over half a century, so I thought that tonight's production would be equal time, right? A night for Nancy. Then I learned of your 1971 pioneering and coeducational Washington press corps. You changed the name. You admitted male members. You also encouraged male speakers. So here I am, a poor but modest substitute for the former Nancy Davis, ready to defend myself and every other middle-aged male in America.

After his opening remarks at the second press conference of his presidency, Reagan said:

And now we shall get on with our first attempt at "Reagan roulette."

Commenting for the first time on the charges brought against his former spokesman, Larry Speakes, for fabricating presidential quotes, Reagan kidded at a press conference:

That's the nice thing about this job. You get to quote yourself shamelessly, and if you don't, Larry Speakes will.

In response to former spokesman Larry Speakes's charge that the President does not read newspapers, Reagan told a group of newspaper reporters:

Yes, I do, so you're not getting away with anything.

—1988

In another press conference in which he was questioned about Speakes's claim that the President preferred news summaries to reading the newspaper, Reagan smiled and told reporters:

I begin with the comics first.

—1988

In response to Larry Speakes's admission that he made up remarks about the 1985 Geneva summit and passed them along to reporters as direct quotations from President Reagan, Reagan said of the things he supposedly said:

I was not aware of it and just heard it recently, as the rest of you did, in the words of [Speakes's] book.

—1988

Reagan told the White House News Photographers Association:

It's not easy having so many photographers around. . . . For instance, I told everybody—my right side is my good side. My far right side. Keeping my right side to the cameras is no problem when I walk home from the Oval Office in the evening. Morning's a different thing. You know what it's like to start the day by walking to the office backwards?

—MAY 15, 1986

ON PERSONAL/FAMILY LIFE

Speaking about his secretary of the treasury, Donald Regan, the President discovered a class distinction in the two Irishmen's names:

Those who called themselves "Reegan" were the lawyers and doctors. It was only the laborers and farmers who called themselves "Raygan."

Of his wife Nancy and Donald Regan, Reagan joked:

Nancy and Don at one point tried to patch things up. They met privately over lunch. Just the two of them and their food tasters.

Reagan had the following conversation with House Speaker Thomas P. O'Neill about President Grover Cleveland and baseball trivia:

Reagan: I have some affection for him. I played Grover Cleveland Alexander in the movies.
O'Neill: Yes, he was one of the fourteen pitchers to win 300 games.
Reagan: Yes, and the 1926 World Series.

—WASHINGTON, D.C.

JANUARY 1981

Reagan remarked at a National Prayer Breakfast held on his birthday:

Nancy and I are delighted to be here and I want to thank you for the day in my life you recognized in starting off my celebration of my thirty-first anniversary of my thirty-ninth birthday.

Reagan attended one evening a dance performance in which his son, Ron, appeared. After the performance the President greeted his son, who was still wearing the Swing Era baggy pants he had worn during the show, joking:

If I had known you would have needed pants like that, I would have saved you a bunch of them.

Reagan remarked at a luncheon with Irish Ambassador Sean Donlon:

You know, I have to tell you, if you don't mind, a personal note. I am deeply grateful for this because my father was orphaned at age six and I grew up never having heard anything or knowing anything about my family tree, and I would meet other people of the name Reagan or Regan—we're all of the same clan, all cousins, but I tried to say to the secretary one day that his branch of the family just couldn't handle that many letters—then received a letter or a paper from Ireland that told me that in the clan to which we belong, those who said Regan and spelled it that way were the professional people and the educators and only the common laborers called it Reagan. So, meet a common laborer.

—WASHINGTON, D.C.
MARCH 17, 1981

The President said the following to the performers in Ford's Theater Gala before the curtain rose:

You know, one of the great benefits we found of living here is you get to be a part of the great history of this beautiful city. Now, I used the word "benefit" there. For some who are among us tonight—you realize that word has a very singular meeting. A benefit in the entertainment world is any occasion where the actors are performing without pay. And I learned at first on such occasions, if you don't sing or dance, you usually wind up introducing someone who does.

I remember one such occasion when there were seven of us lined up to introduce Nelson Eddy singing "Shortenin' Bread." If you did that enough, that usually led to your being an after-dinner speaker. And as that went on, you could talk your way right out of show business into another line of work.

During a speech at a White House reception opening the "Champions of American Sport" Exhibition, Reagan joked about his own sports experience:

I couldn't play baseball because I couldn't see good enough. That's why I turned to football. The ball was bigger, and so were the fellows.

Once during a speech to the building trades, Reagan told this story about his first summer job working for a company that remodeled homes:

There . . . weren't any bulldozers or skip loaders in those days, so the grading was pretty much pick and shovel. I remember one hot morning I'd been swinging pick for about four hours. I heard the noon whistle blow. I had been waiting for that sound. I had the pick over my shoulder ready for the next blow, and when I heard the whistle, I just let go, walked out from underneath it and let it fall behind me. I heard a loud scream and then some very profane language. I turned around, and the boss was standing right behind me. That pick was embedded in the ground right between his feet. Two inches either way and I'd have nailed him.

Reagan often incorporated jokes into his speeches, such as this favorite one about the Soviet Union:

You know, in the Soviet Union, for a private citizen to buy an automobile, there is a ten-year waiting period. . . . You have to put the money down too, ten years in advance.

So this man has gone in and he's doing all the signing, all the papers, and putting out his money.

And finally when he makes that final signature the man behind the counter says, "Now, come back in ten years and take delivery."

And the man asks, "Morning or afternoon?"

And the man behind the counter says, "Well, ten years from now, what difference does it make?"

"Well," the man answers, "the plumber's coming in the morning."

—WORLD AFFAIRS COUNCIL MEETING
1988

Relaying a conversation he had with his chief of staff, Donald Regan, Reagan said:

People are too ready to jump to conclusions. The other day when I told Don Regan I was opposed to dictators, whoever and wherever they are, he asked me if he should start packing.

Reagan on communism:

The strength of the Solidarity movement in Poland demonstrates the truth told in an underground joke in the Soviet Union. It is that the Soviet Union would remain a one-party nation even if an opposition party were permitted because everyone would join the opposition party.

Reagan said the only ethnic jokes he could tell were Irish ones since he was Irish himself. One of his favorites was the story of a gondolier who was singing a popular Neapolitan song as he paddled his boat through the canals. According to Reagan:

The Lord said, "I wonder what would happen if I took away twenty-five percent of his brainpower," as the gondolier was singing "O sole mio." . . .

So the Lord did and the gondolier sang only part of the song, "O sole, O sole."

The Lord said, "Hey, I'll take half of it away," and the gondolier's song was shortened to "O so, O so."

Finally, the Lord said, "What will happen if I take all of his brainpower away?' and he did. And the gondolier suddenly switched his tune and sang, "When Irish Eyes Are Smiling."

Joking with reporters about his talented chief of staff, Donald Regan, Reagan said:

I even follow what you write. One of you just recently wrote a piece questioning why things seemed to be going so well for me. It's just a case of letting Reagan be Regan.

In a speech before the World Affairs Council, Reagan noted that Soviet leader Mikhail Gorbachev "laughed quite heartily" at this joke:

An American and a Russian are arguing about their two countries. And the American said, "Look, I can go into the Oval Office, pound the President's desk and say, 'Mr. President, I don't like the way you're running our country.'"

And the Russian said, "I can do that."

And the American said, "You can?"

And the Russian said, "I can go into the Kremlin, into the general secretary's office, I can pound on his desk and say, 'Mr. General Secretary, I don't like the way President Reagan's running his country.' "

—1988

Reagan remarked outside Angelo's Restaurant in the Little Italy section of New York City:

And now they tell me that they're going to take me inside and feed me. And I heard so much last night about how I'm going to be fed. I haven't had any breakfast yet. I've been waiting for this.

—NEW YORK, N.Y.
MARCH 14, 1981

Reagan summed up his views on communism with this one-liner:

How do you tell a Communist? Well, it's someone who reads Marx and Lenin. And how do you tell an anti-Communist? It's someone who understands Marx and Lenin.

—ARLINGTON, VIRGINIA
SEPTEMBER 25, 1987

When a visiting friend from California was ready to return home, a slightly homesick, and cold (it was February), Ronald Reagan said:

Wait until I get my hat. I'll go with you.

—WASHINGTON, D.C.
FEBRUARY 1981

A friend of mine was asked to a costume ball a short time ago. He slapped some egg on his face and went as a liberal economist.

—FEBRUARY 11, 1988

In some ways working at the White House reminded Reagan of his father's business in Tampico, Illinois. He remarked:

I'm back living above the store again.

After the successful flight of the space shuttle Columbia, *President Reagan was presented with a gold space flight jacket by astronauts Young and Crippen. Reagan asked:*

You won't mind if I only wear this in the earth's atmosphere?

Reagan said in a speech:

And in the rough days ahead, and I know there will be such days, I hope that you'll be like the mother of the young lad in camp—when the camp director told her that he was going to have to discipline her son. And she said, "Well, don't be too hard on him. He's very sensitive. Slap the boy next to him and that will scare Irving."

What are the four things wrong with Soviet agriculture? Spring, summer, autumn, and winter.

Before an interview on National Public Radio, Reagan didn't realize that the microphones were on and joked:

Congress has just approved legislation outlawing Russia forever. We begin bombing in five minutes.

Reagan, whose father was an alcoholic, never told jokes about alcohol abuse. But he did have this one about Gorbachev's anti-drinking campaign:

While visiting a factory . . . Gorbachev is accosted by a worker who demands he defend his much-publicized crack-down on vodka.

"Well, look at it this way. If you had one glass of vodka

before coming to work, would you be able to handle this complex machinery?" Gorbachev asks.

The worker replies that he has never thought about it.

"If you had two glasses of vodka before coming to work, would you be able to discharge any of your responsibilities?" Gorbachev persists.

"If you had three glasses of vodka before coming to work, would you even be able to come to work?" Gorbachev demands.

"Of course," the man replies indignantly. "I'm here, aren't I?"

According to Reagan, Soviet Leader Mikhail Gorbachev enjoyed this joke, which he told in a speech to the World Affairs Council:

You know, less than one family out of seven in the Soviet Union owns an automobile. Most of the automobiles are driven by the bureaucrats—the government furnishes them and drivers and so forth.

So an order went out one day to the police that anyone caught speeding—anyone, no matter who—gets a ticket.

Well, Gorbachev came out of his country home, his dacha; he was late getting to the Kremlin. There was his limousine and driver waiting.

He told the driver to get in the backseat, he'd drive. And down the road he went.

They passed two motorcycle cops. One took out after him, and pretty soon he's back with his buddy. And his buddy says, "Well, did you give him a ticket?" and his buddy says, "No."

"Well," he said, "why not?"

"Oh," the cop said, "too important."

"Well," his buddy said, "we're told to give anybody a ticket, no matter who it is."

"Oh," the cop said, "no, no. This one was too important, I couldn't."

"Well," the buddy said, "who was it?"

"I couldn't recognize him," the cop said. "But his driver was Gorbachev."

—1988

While visiting the Canadian parliament, Reagan—after thanking the Canadians for such exports as Art Linkletter and Mary Pickford—commented on the demonstrators who protested his visit:

[They] must have been imported to make me feel at home.

Reagan on his busy schedule:

I have no time to be President.

The press often remarked on the "father and son" relationship between Reagan and Mike Deaver, assistant to the President. Aware of this view, Reagan said to Deaver at a White House concert:

You can come over here, son, and sit by me.

Speaking to reporters by phone, Reagan said:

Well, I'm up at Camp David. We're getting a little used to it now, but I have to tell you the first time I came to this place, to Camp David, Ed Meese sewed name tags in my undershorts and T-shirts.

The rule says, if it ain't broke, don't fix it.

Reagan told the following story at a luncheon for Baseball Hall of Fame members:

I'm going to tell another story here that has been confirmed for me by Waite Hoyt. Those of you who played when the Dodgers were in Brooklyn, know that Brooklyn-ites have a tendency to refer to someone by the name of Earl as "Oil." But if they want a quart of oil in the car, they say, "Give me a quart of earl." And Waite was sliding into second and he twisted his ankle and instead of getting up he was lying there, and there was a deep hush over the whole ballpark and then a Brooklyn voice was heard above all that silence, "Gee, Hurt is hoyt."

While visiting a school, Reagan joked with a grammar class:

I thought maybe you asked me here to remedial English class because you heard my speeches.

In a speech at the President's Volunteer Action Awards, Reagan opened:

I don't know how many of you stayed up the other night to watch the Academy Awards. I broke a rule and stayed up past midnight. They never called my name.

—April 13, 1983

In a television appearance, Reagan advised the American public:

As I often say, trust everybody, but cut the cards.

One of Reagan's favorite Soviet Union jokes is about a lost parrot and its Russian owner, who tells the Soviet KGB secret police:

In case that bird is found, I just want you to know I disagree with everything it says.

Reagan often told this joke about the USSR:

The party official asks a farmer how things are going, and the farmer replies that the harvest is so bountiful that the potatoes would reach the "foot of God" if piled on top of one another.

"But this is the Soviet Union," says the commissar, "there is no God here." The farmer replies. "That's right, there are no potatoes, either."

After Reagan was elected to his second term in 1984 by a wide margin, he commented on his popularity:

Not bad, not bad.

In a speech on the shores of Lake Michigan, Reagan delivered this spontaneous one-liner:

Being here along the lake reminds me of a story—when you're my age, everything reminds you of a story.

Quoting one of his favorite tales by the eighteenth-century writer Ivan Krylov about a swan, a crawfish, and a pike who were trying to move a wagon, Reagan said:

The swan was flying upward, the crawfish kept crawling backward and the pike kept making for water. The result was, they got nowhere. And the wagon is still there, to this day.

—1987

Reagan's definition of economists:

Economists are people who see something that works in practice and wonder if it would work in theory.

Reagan on his own decision-making philosophy:

The big decisions are simple, but that doesn't mean that they're easy.

According to "Lucky" Roosevelt, who served as Reagan's chief of protocol during his first term, when the President reappointed her for his second term, he sang to her from My Fair Lady, *quoting the section that goes:*

I've grown accustomed to your face.

At a Republican party fund-raiser, Reagan entertained the crowd with a joke he had heard during a recent visit to the Soviet Union:

It's evening in Moscow. A man is walking down the street. A soldier yells "Halt." The man starts to run. The soldier shoots him. Another Russian said to the soldier, "Why did you do that?" The soldier said, "Curfew." [The Man] said, "It isn't curfew yet." (The soldier) said, "I know. He's a friend of mine. I know where he lives. He couldn't have made it."

At a world affairs forum, after pledging efforts to secure talks between Israel and its Arab neighbors, Reagan told his audience:

I can't resist telling you a little joke. It's kind of cynical—very cynical as a matter of fact—about the Middle East.

In the joke, a scorpion comes to a creek and asks a frog to carry him across it, because scorpions can't swim.

The frog says, "Why, you'd sting me if I did."

The scorpion responds, "That'd be silly because if I stung you and you died, I'd drown."

Well, that made sense to the frog so he said, "Get on" and started to ferry him across and in midstream the scorpion stung him.

As both were dying, the frog asked the scorpion, "Why did you do that—now we're both going to die."

And the scorpion said, "This is the Middle East."

—1988

Reagan told an audience the following story about a third-grade teacher who was trying to teach her students the importance of staying warm during the winter:

As the story went, [the teacher's] little brother . . . went out on his sled, stayed out too long, caught cold, then pneumonia, and three days later he was dead. When she finished with the tale there was silence in the room. She thought she had really gotten through to them when a voice in the back said, "Where's his sled?"

One of Reagan's favorite jokes about himself and Gorbachev:

They had me in . . . [a] limousine, with General Secretary Gorbachev, and the head of my Secret Service unit, and his chief security person. And we were . . . sightseeing.

And we pulled up by a waterfall. And supposedly we got out of the car to look at the waterfall and Gorbachev said to my Secret Service man, "Go ahead, jump, go over the fall."

And he said, "I've got a wife and three kids!"

So Gorbachev turned to his own man, and said, "Jump, go over the waterfall." And he did.

Well, my man scrambled down the rocks around the bottom and found the fellow wringing out his clothes, and apparently all right.

And he said, "Well, when he told you to jump and go over the falls—why did you do that?"

And the Soviet said, "I've got a wife and three kids!"

In another Soviet joke, Reagan told the story of an American who tells a Russian that he can stand in front of the White House and yell, "To hell with Ronald Reagan!"

The Russian replies, "That's nothing, I can stand in front of the Kremlin and yell, 'To hell with Ronald Reagan,' too."

CHAPTER 9

The Assassination Attempt

Perhaps one of the truest tests of Ronald Reagan's sense of humor was the horror of the assassination attempt on March 30, 1981. But throughout it all, Reagan always found a reason to keep smiling. That smile not only helped the President through this difficult time but also put the nation's mind at ease.

One of the doctors who treated the President said that Reagan's humor "made him more natural and easier to approach as a patient." And, indeed, his lighthearted quips relaxed all Americans. The moment reports were released of his joking with the nurses and doctors in George Washington University Hospital, the public knew he was all right.

—APRIL 22, 1981

I knew from the manner in which I was unclothed that I probably wouldn't wear that suit again.

—April 22, 1981

Soon after Reagan awoke, presidential aide Lyn Nofziger reported to Reagan, "You'll be happy to know that the government is running normally." The President replied without hesitation:

What makes you think I'd be happy about that?

—April 2, 1981

Reflecting on the shooting, Reagan said:

I guess it goes with the territory.

—Washington, D.C.
March 31, 1981

Reagan wrote in a note to doctors:

Send me to L.A., where I can see the air I'm breathing.

Reagan remarked to an aide:

I really screwed up the schedule.

When Reagan's California allergist, Dr. Ralph Bookman, stopped by his hospital room, the President told him:

Doc, you should have tested me for lead!
—APRIL 12, 1981

I found out it hurts to get shot.

Reagan replied to the doctor who told him that he was a good patient:

I have to be. My father-in-law is a doctor.

Reagan said to his aides assembled at his hospital bedside:

Hi, fellas. I knew it would be too much to hope that we could skip a staff meeting.

In a note to one of his early morning nurses, Reagan wrote:

If I knew I had such talent for this, I'd have tried it sooner.

While in the hospital, Reagan used the excuse of having to use the toilet to give himself a cool sponge bath. Although he fooled the hospital staff, he was worried about being discovered:

I thought they'd find out because I'd made such a mess, so I got down on my hands and knees and mopped up the floor so the nurse wouldn't find out.

After waking from surgery, Reagan scribbled:

I'm still alive, aren't I?

Reagan asked of the man accused of shooting him:

Does anybody know what that guy's beef was?

*The President was overjoyed to learn that Secret Service agent
Timothy J. McCarthy, Officer Thomas K. Delahanty of the
District of Columbia Police, and White House Press Secretary
Jim Brady were improving after being shot:*

That's great news, just great, especially about Jim. We'll
have to get four bedpans and have a reunion.

Reagan quipped to his wife, Nancy:

Honey, I forgot to duck.

*Not realizing that he had been shot, President Reagan first
thought that the Secret Service agent's efforts to get him into the
limousine were too forceful. He commented:*

I've got to apologize to that guy. I accused him of
breaking my ribs.

If I'd gotten this much attention in Hollywood, I never
would have left.

Reagan replied to a nurse who told him, "Keep up the good work!"

You mean this may happen several times more?

The President wanted to make sure that his surgeons were qualified:

I hope you're all Republicans.

Reagan pointed out another misfortune of the attempt to his daughter Maureen:

Ruined one of my best suits.

After entering the hospital, the President queried an attractive nurse:

Does Nancy know about us?

I always heal fast.

In a note to his doctors, Reagan quoted Winston Churchill:

There is no more exhilarating feeling than being shot without result.

—APRIL 28, 1981

After being released from the hospital, Reagan reported to the American people:

Thanks to some very fine people, my health is much improved. I'd like to be able to say that with regard to the health of the economy.

While in the hospital Reagan scribbled the following, paraphrasing W. C. Fields:

All in all, I'd rather be in Philadelphia.

—WASHINGTON, D.C.
MARCH 30, 1981

While recovering back at the White House, Reagan said:

I don't think I'm going to hurdle any tables in the room here for a while.

The day after the assassination attempt, Reagan quipped:

Don't worry. I'll get out of this.

Reagan said to the newly elected White House Press Association president, Clifford Evans:

As one President to another, let me give you some advice. When someone tells you to get into the car, do it—quickly.

Reagan told a reporter who asked, "What are you going to do first when you get home, Mr. President?":

Sit down.

—April 11, 1981

Reagan said of the others who had been shot:

I didn't want a supporting cast.

—WASHINGTON, D.C.
MARCH 31, 1981

Reagan's first public appearance after the assassination attempt was before a joint session of Congress. He received a tumultuous standing ovation.

Thank you. You wouldn't want to talk me into an encore?

—WASHINGTON, D.C.
APRIL 28, 1981

In a speech before Congress, Reagan said:

The society we heard from is made up of millions of compassionate Americans and their children, from college age to kindergarten.

As a matter of fact, as evidence of that I have a letter with me. The letter came from Peter Sweeney. He's in the second grade in the Riverdale School in Rockville Center. And he said: "I hope you get well quick for you might have to make a speech in your pajamas."

And he added a postscript: "P.S. If you have to make a speech in your pajamas, I warned you."

—WASHINGTON D.C.

After the assassination attempt, Reagan usually had a joke to make about anything that sounded like a gunshot. Once in the midst of a speech to the Republican National Convention, a balloon popped. Without missing a beat, he joked:

Missed me.

CHAPTER 10

After the Presidency

The end of Reagan's political career did not mean the end of his relationship with the American people. Reagan charmed America even after he left the Oval Office. He has continued to play a part in the political world, but as his interests have expanded, so too has his material for jokes. From jokes about his harmonica playing to his feelings about postpresidential life, Ronald Reagan is still making America smile.

Referring to Democratic nominee Bill Clinton, Reagan said:

This fellow they've nominated claims he's the new Thomas Jefferson. Well let me tell you something; I knew Thomas Jefferson. He was a friend of mine and Governor . . . you're no Thomas Jefferson!

—REPUBLICAN NATIONAL CONVENTION

1992

After the presidency, Reagan took up the harmonica. When TV journalist Connie Chung got word of the President's new hobby, she expressed her hope that she could film one of his harmonica lessons for her newsmagazine. Reagan replied:

You're the second person to inquire about my harmonica playing ability—or lack thereof. Unfortunately, I'm not taking music lessons and probably should be. I've always liked the harmonica, but can barely play a tune. My repertoire is limited to "Red River Valley" and I play for my own self—amusement exclusively—usually when I don't have my hearing aids in.

At a Republican gala held during Clinton's presidency, Reagan said:

I must say that returning to Washington today really brought back memories. As our plane headed toward the airport, I looked down on the White House, and it was just like the good old days . . . the South Lawn, the Rose Garden . . . David Gergen. I looked over a couple of blocks, and there was the Internal Revenue Service—bigger than I ever remembered it. When I looked down at the enormous United States Post Office building I could just see the excitement on the faces of the bureaucrats—knowing they would soon be managing our national health care system! Up on Capitol Hill, I saw that big, white dome, bulging with new tax revenues. I instinctively reached for my veto pen and thought to myself, "Go ahead, make my day." You may have seen President Clinton draw his own veto pen on television just last week. The difference is that his pen doesn't have any ink in it! Unless, of course, you're talking about red ink. And we all know the Democrats have plenty of that!

—1994

After watching President Bill Clinton's State of the Union address, former President Reagan said at a Republican gala:

I'm reminded of the old adage that imitation is the sincerest form of flattery. Only in this case, it's not flattery, but grand larceny: the intellectual theft of ideas that you and I recognize as our own. Speech delivery counts for little on the world stage unless you have convictions, and, yes, the vision to see beyond the front row seats.

—FEBRUARY 3, 1994

When you see all that rhetorical smoke billowing up from the Democrats, well, ladies and gentlemen, I'd follow the example of their nominee; don't inhale.

—REPUBLICAN NATIONAL CONVENTION
1992

During the 1988 presidential campaign, Reagan kidded:

With everyone following the presidential campaign, I've been feeling a little bit lonely. I've been so desperate for attention, I almost considered holding a news conference.